DCPL0000068466

# TILL WE MEET AGAIN

Mick Grimes

D1340694

TILL WE MEET AGAIN
Mick Grimes

Copyright © Mick Grimes 2008

Michael Grimes has asserted his right under the Copyright, Designs and Patents Act, 1988 to be recognised as the author of this work.

This book is sold subject to the condition that it shall not, by way of trade or otherwise, be lent, resold, hired out, or otherwise circulated without the author's prior consent in any form of binding or cover other than that in which it is published and without a similar condition including this being imposed on the subsequent purchaser.

Book design by Fiona Martin.
Printed by Ecclesville Printing Services,
178 Ecclesville Road, Fintona, Co. Tyrone.
Published by Cregg Publishing.

ISBN 978-0-9559956-0-6
A CIP catalogue record for this book is available from the British Library.

DEDICATION

I wish to dedicate this book to my wife Mary, my daughter Avril Monaghan, her daughter Maura and her unborn twins, and to all those who lost their lives in the Omagh Bomb tragedy on the 15th August 1998.

## ACKNOWLEDGEMENTS

I would very much like to acknowledge and thank each and every one who provided material, information, stories or pictures that are contained in this book. This would be difficult as many of the pictures were sent in for publication in the 'Link' magazine many years ago. A number of those who contributed are no longer with us. The list would be long, and inevitably incomplete. I sincerely hope that a short list of names will not offend the good people who helped but whose names are not listed.

I would like to thank all the Aherne family, but especially Con, who although wheelchair bound was our guide and source of information over the years on countless journeys. Pat McSorley of Rainbow Graphics for giving generously of his time and talent. Miss Susan McNamee for her thesis 'The Birth of the Great Northern Railway in Tyrone'. Samuel McDowell for identifying the land over which the races were run and for the details of the last meeting. Fiona Martin for the cover design and typesetting. Jack Woods and Hugh Ward for their advice and encouragement. All of the family members who helped in different ways, especially Susan who came to my assistance at every beck and call, Ferghal and Damien for scanning and editing photographs. Sinead and Niall deserve a special mention for the long hours they spent proof reading the text and making it presentable for the printers.

To all these people and many more I am deeply indebted.

## POEMS

CHAPTERS

PREFACE

Readers may ask why a retired farmer would wish to sit down and try to write a book. Well, for the reason we will have to go back almost thirty years. About that time the youth club in Beragh, a small village near Omagh in County Tyrone, was going strong and at one committee meeting it was proposed that it might be a good idea if the club would produce a weekly newssheet. The motion was adopted and soon after the newssheet, titled 'Link', was launched and was an immediate success. For a time articles for publication came in thick and fast and filling the pages was not difficult. But as weeks passed by suitable text became scarce. On one occasion when text was in short supply I was asked by our editor, Fr. Jim Carroll, to produce a few lines of farming news. Now, it was over twenty years since I had left primary school, just few weeks before my fourteenth birthday. It is easy to understand why my grasp of English fell far short of that required for journalism, but when I produced a few lines of rhyme that helped to fill the page I was asked to make sure we had a quantity of space fillers available each week.

It was about a year later on a Christmas morning that I found a bulky envelope amongst my presents. It was from Mary, my wife, and my daughter Avril. On opening it I found a small book, well presented and professionally bound. It contained all the little so-called poems or rhymes I had written up to that date. It was good to know that some one cared.

On different occasions in the years that followed Mary sometimes hinted that I should try to write a book. While I did not turn down the idea point blank I knew in my heart that it was beyond my capability. Then in the years after the Omagh atrocity in 1998 the fact that I had made no effort to comply with my wife's request sometimes caused me concern. About eighteen months ago I decided to make an attempt. No doubt some readers will frown at my endeavour but I like to think that somewhere beyond the great divide there is one who smiles.

8

# School Days

The sun was still low in the sky on a showery spring morning away back in 1932. It was not yet nine o'clock but my father and his helper, a man called Johnnie, were having their breakfast after completing their chores in the yard and before going to work on the roads. A shower had just passed over and the sun emerged from behind a dark cloud casting long shadows over the wet ground. It shone straight at the door of our home in the townland of Laragh and a beam of sunlight passed through a small slit between the boards and shimmered on a floor tile close to where a kitten was lapping up some milk. The playful kitten stretched out a paw to touch or catch the ray, but when the light shone on its outstretched limb, the second paw came into action and soon the kitten was lying on its back with all four feet trying to grasp the ray of light. Seconds later a dark cloud again blocked out the sun and the ray of light disappeared. The amazed kitten got to its feet, paused for a time, before strolling up close to the hearth fire and stretched out for a sleep. When the shower passed the sun reappeared, as did the ray of light through the slit in the door, but this time it shone on a different tile.

I brought this to the attention of my father and Johnnie. They told me that if I were to sit down and put a mark on the floor every five minutes as the sun moved in the sky I would have a sundial and we would not need a clock. This I couldn't understand as I was only five years old and it was to be my first day at school. I was all dressed up in short navy blue trousers and a lighter coloured blue shirt, both skilfully made by my mother from sections of material salvaged from part-worn garments. In the 1930s no useful rem-

Leabharlanna Poibli Chathair Bhaile Átha Cliath

Dublin City Public Libraries

nant of cloth was thrown in the ragbag until all seams were ripped, the buttons removed and carefully stored in the press to be used for remodelling or when patches were required.

Not all the activities or new experiences of my first day at school are clear in my mind but a few remain deeply engraved and are unlikely to be eroded. My first sighting of the old lady teacher, as she endeavoured to light the fire in the old Stanley range, never seems to fade. Clad entirely in black with her frock sleeves pulled up above her elbows, surrounded by a bucket of coal, some damp bog fir and a can of paraffin oil, she set about the task. She poured some oil on the fir before putting it into the firebox. Then, after placing the lumps of coal on top, she poured in some more oil. From a drawer in the table she took a box of matches, and after striking one, she stood well back and dropped it into the range. Flames and black smoke shot high into the room for some time before she managed to get the lid in place. This partially subdued the blaze but smoke still poured out from the many cracks and through the front bars of the old range. Gradually the flames died down and the smoke stopped. When it was evident that the fire was completely out the lid was removed. A further quantity of oil was poured in and another match applied. Again we had smoke and flames for a few moments, but this time, before the fire was completely out, the lid was removed and a third helping of oil was applied. Flames sprang to a record height but fortunately the fire did hold and the teacher, whose hands, arms and face were now black with soot, ordered us to sit quietly in our seats while she went to wash up. Her home or residence was a semi-detached part of the school where she lived with her husband and family.

Already I had gained two new experiences. In my young life I had never seen a lump of coal nor had I seen a fire being lit in this way. At home our fire was never completely extinguished. Each night the fire was raked. The burning turf and a couple of fresh sods were placed together and covered with ashes. In the morning, when the ashes were removed, there were always enough embers to start the fire for the new day. Some homes boasted that their fire had never been allowed to go out for a decade and a few would claim that theirs had been kept alive for over a century.

*Mrs McGrath pictured above with 40 of her pupils at Beragh National School 1930.*
*My two elder sisters, Brigie and Maggie, are sitting in the second row, second and third from the right.*

In my school days it was seldom that there was a box of matches in our house. Small strips were torn from a dry fir block, tied together and hung near the fire. These were used as lamplighters. When outside fires were to be lit, a few coals from the hearth were placed in an old bucket and carried to where they were required. In my earliest days at school we had no electric or mains water supply. The nearest pump was in a neighbour's yard about one hundred yards away. An enamel mug hung on top and in the summer time there was always a queue of children, some thirsty, others just enjoying a few moments freedom.

The classroom as I first saw it had four proper school seats or benches which held six or eight pupils each. There was one each for infants, first, second and third classes. New beginners were required to sit on 'forms', long benches with no back support or rest for your books or slate. Periodically fourth class pupils moved into the next room, the master's room, and new beginners got into proper seats. Even slates were in short supply in my young days; perhaps there were half a dozen proper slates, while other children had to be content with a piece of black lino cut into the shape of a slate.

Although the old schoolteacher, who was well past retiring age when I knew her, may not have been an expert at kindling a fire, she had many excellent qualities and we were told that in her prime she was an outstanding teacher. At my introduction to her on my first day at school I told her about the kitten. She said she had not got any cat and would like one but seemed a bit surprised when I brought her two nice white kittens in a basket the following morning. Unfortunately, kittens reared in a barn at a farmyard do not thrive well in a small village house and their lifespan was short. The old lady retired and left the village a short time after I started school.


## School days

*My mother made a suit for me,*
*My shoes were bright and new,*
*When I started school in April*
*In nineteen thirty two.*

*Two big sisters held my hands,*
*We had to walk a mile.*
*If we met a horse and cart,*
*We walked in single file.*

*The teacher used some coal and oil,*
*To make the fire blaze,*
*We burned turf upon the hearth,*
*Back in those happy days.*

*I learned to write upon a slate,*
*'Twas chalk we used back then,*
*I'd gone to school for three long years,*
*Before I got a pen.*

*We dipped the pen nib into ink,*
*'Twas easy smudge the page,*
*Blots made the teacher angry,*
*And set her in a rage.*

*One blot earned us a scolding,*
*But for two it meant the cane,*
*And a warning what would happen,*
*If we smudged the page again.*

*The windows in our classroom,*
*Were in the wall so high,*
*I could see the white clouds floating,*
*And watch the wild birds fly.*

*How I longed for freedom,*
*And kept pining for the day,*
*When I'd last pack my school books,*
*And throw the bag away.*

My next teacher was also a very kind lady, only two or three years from retirement age, whose endearment to the pupils in her care prompted her to take on tasks far beyond the call of duty. It should be noted that during the 1930s poverty was rife in towns, villages and countryside alike. Many children were undernourished and this fact did not go unnoticed by Mrs Rafferty, our new teacher. Quietly and without fuss she arranged with local farmers and gardeners for a daily supply of vegetables suitable for soup making. A butcher of her acquaintance provided a soup bone or suitable piece of meat. The parish supplied other ingredients and condiments. Each morning a large pot or saucepan and a big kettle were put on the range and filled with water. Then, with what seemed little effort, the mistress could attend to the soup making, keep thirty plus children busy at their lessons, and often attend to a new beginner in distress. By lunchtime the soup was ready. Every child was obliged to bring his or her bowl or cup. Soup was provided for pupils in both rooms, sixty or seventy children in all. Mrs Rafferty measured out the soup and the girls in the senior classes acted as waitresses. They were also expected to help with the washing up. The entire operation took about a quarter of an hour, leaving us fifteen minutes for play. On Fridays we got a cup of cocoa instead of soup.

A rod was used for slapping but only in extreme cases. I once found myself in that category but when my misdemeanour came to light, no rod could be found. For a time I thought I might be spared but further investigations uncovered more deception. It should be noted that in my schooldays Biro pens had not yet been invented. We used pens with nibs that we dipped into the inkwells in our desk. If we dipped in too deep when the inkwell was full the nib was likely to take too much ink and drops would fall on the page of our book. This happened all too often in my case and since each blot was most likely to earn a slap, I often neglected to hand up my book for correction. On a particular day when I thought my writing was reasonable I did present it for inspection but unfortunately the teacher got suspicious and turned back the pages. It was then that my crime came to light.

For a moment she gazed at me as if in disbelief. Then she opened the drawer of the table and took out a penknife, which she gave to me and ordered me to go out and bring in a good rod. Now at home it was not unusual to be sent out on that errand but seldom for a rod to beat oneself. Dutifully on this occasion I picked a rod and presented it to the teacher. She commented that it was a good one but a little bit short. Catching it by the very end she gave me one good smack. She turned over another couple of pages and was about to strike again when blood started to drip from her hand. The jagged end of the rod had punctured the delicate skin on the palm of her hand and the poor lady had to be taken to hospital to have the bleeding stopped. We got the evening off. I felt really guilty when she was not at school next day. The incident was not mentioned again but when she returned I think I could truthfully say we became better friends. Soon after it was time to move to the master's room.

Already a younger member of the family had started school and became the teacher's pet. On one occasion he caused a period of awkward silence when he asked the teacher why all the hair on her head moved when she scratched her head with a pencil. Wigs were uncommon in those days.

## *Teach the Children*

*Teach the children God gave you to care*
*To love one another and all his gifts share*
*Let no word or action cause others grief or pain*
*Should somebody fall, we'll help them rise again.*

*How can we, before it is too late*
*Cast aside the curse of war and hate*
*Then hope that conflict in the world would cease*
*And we can all rejoice in love and peace*

*Just teach the children God gave you to care*
*To love one another and all his gifts share*
*Let no word or action cause others grief or pain*
*Should somebody fall, we'll help them rise again.*

*Where must we search, if peace we hope to find*
*True peace that is, in every heart and mind*
*Peace that gives each one the right to work and rest*
*And for the love of God, does love his neighbour best*

*Just teach the children God gave you to care*
*To love one another and all his gifts share*
*Let no word or action cause others grief or pain*
*Should somebody fall, we'll help them rise again.*

After four years at school the thought of having to move to the master's room was a shock to the system. In the days prior to the changeover we were constantly reminded of the fate that awaited us. The wood panelled partition that separated the rooms did little to quell the sound. We were well aware of the thick leather strap that was used instead of the rod, as well as the strength of the arm that wielded it. A nudge or a frightened glance from an equally terrified classmate made sure we shared in the pain of every slap or act of chastisement dished out in the master's room. To make matters worse, senior pupils from that room made sure we got an inflated version of how punishment was administered.

When the dreaded day arrived we found out that it was not as bad as we were led to believe. We did have to endure many a good thrashing in the first year or so but then there were privileges. We got to play football with the big boys. First to do goals, and when one showed enough courage to tackle a very big boy or a bully, we could get our place on the team.

Football had its season. So too had the marbles. We had ordinary marbles and 'taws', big 'dabbers' and 'glassies'. We were not allowed to crawl about on our knees playing marbles as it destroyed the toes of our boots. Sometimes we played 'pitch and toss'. Since we had no money we used tin tops. These were the tops of lemonade or mineral bottles. Even they were scarce. In the autumn we played chestnuts or 'conkers'. But most of all we looked forward to the winter when we would have snow for snowballing and sleighing, and a hard frost so that we could have a good slide. Sliding on the ice was the best fun of all. Half worn hobnailed boots were great on a good slide. The toilets at our school were at the foot of a steep hill. A narrow path led down to them. On one particular hard winter it became covered with hard snow and ice. We used it as a toboggan run. I remember the master standing straddle legged over the path at the top and giving every child a good shove as he or she sat down on a piece of wood or the branch of a palm tree. Some used an old bag while others cut up an old carpet. If someone capsized on the way down, many more would bump into him or her. Soon there would be a tangled heap of arms and legs, shouting and screaming, bumps and bruises but no complaints.

*Master Conway and the pupils of Beragh National School 1948*

About the same time we had a great slide on the main road at the Chapel brae[1]. This brae was levelled when the road was being straightened. On a particular day a bunch of schoolboys were sliding when Packie McMackin, the blacksmith's son, came from the village carrying two long bars of iron on his shoulder. He started at the top of the hill and intended to slide to the bottom. At the same time a lad from the senior class said he was going for a 'hunker'. A hunker meant sliding on one's left foot in an almost sitting position, with the right foot sticking out in front. As he passed

Packie, he managed to tip him on the heel and put him off balance. Watching the manoeuvres of Packie going down the hill was entertaining. Still clutching the bars of iron with his right hand he made gigantic circles and designs in the air with his left arm. Sometimes he would lift his right foot high in the air, then suddenly change to his left as he sped down the steep incline. Torville and Dean in their prime could not have outclassed his performance. At the bottom of the hill he overshot the end of the slide and landed, still upright, out in the deep snow. We refrain from putting his remarks in print, and maybe it was just coincidence that the lad who played the prank left for America soon after leaving school and has only returned on a couple of occasions.

With the volume of traffic now on our roads it is hard to believe that there was a time when it was safe to allow twenty or more children to make a slide on the main road. This slide was kept in good shape for days by pouring buckets of water down the hill last thing at night. More surprisingly, it was quite close to the police barracks. Two or three policemen manned the barrack. Sergeant Murray, who lived across the way with his wife and family, was noted for being extremely strict. On a lovely summer's day two of his daughters who were about my age, and two older girls, walked out past our house which was only a short distance from the village. We were playing in the nearby bog and they came to join us. Playing in the bog usually meant jumping from the bog bank out over a pool of water which was about four foot wide. The height of the bank was seven or more foot high and when we landed our bare feet would sink deep in the soft bog. The village girls thought it was too high and would not jump so we moved to a spot where the bank was only four foot high. Here all joined in the fun except Angela, the elder of the two sisters. She would run to the edge but was afraid to jump. I was nearby when she made her fourth attempt and as she was about to stop, I gave her a wee shove. She still did not jump but fell on her face, down in the mud below. Luckily it was not too deep, but very little soft peat makes a nasty mess of a flimsy white summer frock. I was only about eight years old at the time. I stayed in the bog long after all the others had gone home that evening. When I did venture into the house there was a deafening silence for a while. Then I was told that Sergeant Murray would be out to get me and he would put me in the black hole. When he did not come I was told he would get me when I would go back to school. The black hole was a small dark cell with a steel door, often underground, where drunk or rowdy people were kept over-night or until they were taken to a proper prison. There was a black hole in most towns and villages, especially where fairs or markets were held. About this time a new barrack was built at the other end of the village and all the police moved there. Shortly afterwards Sergeant Murray was transferred and I think it was Sergeant McConville who replaced him.

From an early age we were given little jobs to do when we got home from school. Taking in enough turf to keep the fire going until next evening was a job for three of us. Two carried the basket between them from the shed and emptied the turf on the kitchen floor. A third one built them up in the turf corner, a little cove near the fire. The duties rotated each evening so that every third evening we were entitled to stay inside and build the turf up neatly. We would stand up on a stool when the building got too high.

As we grew older we were given the job of washing the potatoes which were boiled to feed the pigs, turkeys, hens and sometimes the ducks. In the springtime the ducks fended for themselves. They ran in the furrows after the horses and plough and gobbled up worms until they could eat no more. Years later, when the first tractors started ploughing, the ducks were a nuisance as the tractors moved faster, the furrows were deeper and the ducks were unable to get out of the way. The driver often had to stop and lift them out. Indeed, as the tractor driver also had to watch the plough which was on the rear of the tractor, it was inevitable that some ducks were killed and were buried in a short space of time. In such cases the fox was often blamed.

Another hateful after school job was putting the turkeys into their house on late November and early December evenings. The turkeys had to be put in before dark. As there was no window in the house in which they were kept, we had to leave the door open and stand there so that they had light to fly up onto the roosts. Most flew up immediately when they went inside, but the last couple often kept us standing a long time. Moreover, as the last one flew up it sometimes knocked others down, which prolonged our stand at the door.

On Saturdays we helped to carry out the chairs and table to the yard where they were scrubbed, while the floor of the kitchen was being washed. If necessary the white wash on the walls was renewed. In my early teen years my after school duties changed to ensuring there was hay in the horse's manger and two buckets of water ready at the stable door for the horse to drink when he came in from work. His stall had to be properly cleaned and bedded with a measure of oats near at hand to put in his feeding box when the harness was removed. Each item of harness was hung on its own special peg but the collar was taken into the kitchen and hung near the fire. This was the custom in most farmhouses as the collar was often wet with sweat.

The thought of going back to school after the summer holidays was vexing to say the least. Worse still we were compelled to wear shoes after romping barefooted since the first day of May. It helped a little if we got a new pair, but more often than not our old ones were repaired, or we had to be content with a pair of hand-me-downs. The shoes we wore to school were strong hob-nailed ones. If they needed repairs we took them to Alex McFarland, or "Black Alex" as he was more commonly known. Each of us did have a pair of fine shoes, or as we called them, Sunday shoes. If these needed repair they were taken to Christie Wilkinson.

I am sure that records will show that wellington boots were available much earlier but the first pair of rubber wellingtons in our district were purchased by the man who lived on the farm next to ours when I was still a young schoolboy. They were a kind of novelty at first and he seldom wore them himself, but lent them to the neighbours who were cleaning 'sheughs' [2] or drains. Very soon all farmers and farm workers procured wellingtons for themselves.

Even rubber tyres and tubes for cars, lorries and bicycle wheels were relatively new back then and a couple of vehicles which had solid rubber bands or tyres were locally owned. One such lorry, belonging to Scott's of Omagh, was delivering material at Sixmilecross Co-op in 1934 when the driver reversed the truck down towards the steep entry. Later when he attempted to move off he was unable to do so as the steel rims spun round inside the hard solid rubber tyres. Another lorry had to be summoned to tow the vehicle to level ground.

# Laragh

Close to Beragh village in the heart of sweet Tyrone,
There stands a sentinel sycamore near an ancient standing stone,
Then the wee road wends on westwards till it meets a rippling stream,
'Twas there I spent my childhood days, 'tis the focus of my dream.

Around our home in Laragh, sheltered low beneath the hill,
Every bush and stone and pathway, I see them clearly still,
The drifting snows of Winter, the first green shoots of Spring,
The hay-days in the Summer time and the fruits that Autumn bring.

Sparrows nesting in the thatch above the old green door,
The dresser laden down with delph, the rough tiled kitchen floor,
Hams of salty bacon hang from the ceiling timbers,
And I still think that I can smell spuds toasting in the cinders.

The walls are freshly whitened and the chairs are scrubbed and clean
The salt box hangs just at the hob, that's where it's always been,
The tongs are by the fireside, there's socks slung on the crane,
And a wee small floral curtain on the kitchen window pane.

The horse's collar hanging on its special wooden peg,
There's a folded piece of cardboard 'neath the table's shortest leg,
Two enamelled buckets full of water from the spring,
While around the hearthstone the crickets chirp and sing.

The churn is in its usual place beside the pantry door,
Over in the corner is the broom that sweeps the floor,
There's a ten stone poke of flour sitting on a 'bunty' chair,
And a rod that helps to keep the peace when daddy isn't there.

We always knew the night each week when 'céilíers'³ would call,
We'd know them ere they'd lift the latch by the sound of their footfall,
We'd quietly sit and listen to every word they said,
We knew that if we made a sound we'd be skedaddled off to bed.

The nights that Uncle George came I remember them so well,
He smoked Warhorse tobacco and we used to love the smell,
'Twas strange the way he lit the pipe, he'd put tobacco in the bowl,
He'd take the tongs in his other hand and light it with a coal.

He had a dog called Daisy that followed him about,
A cow had kicked it when 'twas young and its tongue kept falling out.
Aunt Brigid came along with him if it was a Sunday night.
There'd be some nice sweet things to eat and that was our delight.

Joe Fenton was another man that called with us each week
He'd use the words we'd say in prayer, quite often when he'd speak.
The things he'd say were awkward and don't fit well in rhyme,
His yarns I still remember, they do not fade with time.

The fires burned to embers on a chilly winter's night,
We'd see the shadows dancing, in the oil lamp's flickering light,
Mother's quietly knitting, dad's sleeping in his chair,
Now it's almost bedtime, so we all join in a prayer.

Then before retiring the fire we would rake.
Soon all would be quiet, save the aul' cow at the stake.
Maybe in the stable the horse would scratch his heel,
Or the sow would think 'twas feeding time and we'd hear the litter squeal.

But things are not the same just now, as they were in days of yore,
There is no salt box near the hob, no sparrows o'er the door,
The hams of bacon can't be seen, nor do the crickets sing.
The water gushes from a tap, not carried from a spring.

The cattle feed on silage now, and tractors pull the ploughs,
And huge machines in dairies can milk big herds of cows.
But the little stream still ripples by our old-time childhood home,
And still the sentinel sycamore stands beside the ancient standing stone.

# Feathered Friends

A ridge of high ground in the fields behind our house hindered our view northwards. To the front and just beyond the road Beragh Hill rose steep and high. Even the winter sun failed to peep over the top and remove the artistic designs left on the windows by the previous night's frost.

The little burn ran eastwards down the valley towards the village which was just out of sight around the bend. Two small fields away to the west the old bog road ran like a massive ten foot high dyke between bog and farm land. It also seemed to act as a boundary line for birds and beasts. In the hedgerows between the fields and along the road blackbirds and thrushes, finches and wrens found ample space for nesting. Robins and yellow-hammers (we knew them as yellow-yourlings) chose the mossy banks. The sparrows felt at home in the eaves of the thatched roof. Blue tits disappeared into the small crevices in the stone walls of the barn and the swallows returned each year to their nests in the turf shed. Pigeons seemed content with 'two sticks across and a little bit of moss' in any old tree, while the magpie built a bulky, covered nest high up in some tree which was difficult to climb.

Across the bog road in the area where the turf had been cut, many different species of birds made their home, but here all nests were on the ground. Peewits (lapwings) and curlews swooped down noisily at the head of any man or beast who ventured near their nest. Waterfowl laid and hatched their eggs on little islands of reeds out in the many water logged patches. Snipes too nested in the marshy patches. On warm summer evenings, just at dusk, their lonely bleat could be heard as they ascended high into the sky and then suddenly dived earthwards. We never knew if the bleating noise was made with their wings or their beaks. Wagtails often made their nests in the heaps of old turf lying in the bog.

But while each species of bird had its own special charm or song, none could match that of the skylark. Here on the fringe of the bog land these little birds seemed to queue up awaiting clearance for time and space in the clear blue sky. Often, when enjoying our tea while working at the turf, we would see them ascend until they vanished from sight in the cloudless sky, there to add their voice to the harmonious melody which drifted back to earth.

## Our Feathered Friends

*In a mossy bank on his cosy nest*
*The robin shows his scarlet breast.*

*The chaffinch's nest is hard to see*
*Camouflaged in a mossy tree.*

*When wagtails hop along the ground*
*Their longish tails bob up and down.*

*Tom-tits build in a stone wall*
*We seldom see their nest at all.*

*The pigeon builds a scanty nest*
*Four sticks and moss will do the best.*

*The waterhen can wade or swim*
*It nests in reeds quite near the brim.*

*The snipe, I've seldom seen its nest*
*By its long beak I know it best.*

The peewit has a little crest
It likes the marshy ground the best.

The thrush is noted for its song
He'll come quite close but won't stay long

The cuckoo comes but once a year
And when he comes he brings great cheer

We hear the owl hoot late at night
He shies away in broad daylight

The blackbird strikes a special note
With yellow beak and jet black coat

When sparrows nested in the thatch
We waited for their eggs to hatch

Some jackdaws' nests must get quite hot
They sometimes build in a chimney pot

Swallows come and swallows go
It's clear that they don't like the snow.

The corncrake makes a craking sound
It lays its eggs upon the ground.
Farm machines forced it away
We hope it will return some day

The crows or rooks build rookeries
In the very tallest trees
The little ones are rocked at ease
When blows the gentle summer breeze

Starlings are the noisiest birds
The cheekiest of all,
They build in any crevice
In the roof or in the wall

The curlews have got very scarce
But we hope they come again
We often thought their lonely call
Was heralding the rain

But the bird that sings the best
Rises from its little nest
And soars into a cloudless sky
No longer seen with naked eye
Still its song floats back to earth
Bringing joy and bliss and mirth
To all who have the wish to hear
The lark's sweet song so pure and clear.

# Beragh Village

In my schooldays Beragh village had one long straight street with just about fifty houses on each side. Two narrow roads ran out on the north side. On each of these roads there were three or four small houses and a pump which supplied water for all villagers who had not got a pump in their own yard. Not surprisingly, these two roads were known as the Upper and Lower Well Lanes. We were told that the village was designed and built in the 1770s by the late Lord Lowrey-Curry, the then Earl of Belmore. In all the years that had followed little change seemed to have taken place.

In the second half of the 1800s my grandmother went to school in a building near to the lower end of the town. Then, in 1875, the National School was built beside the chapel. For just over a century thereafter, hundreds of children from the village and surrounding area were to receive their education within its walls. In the late 1970s the two-roomed building was deemed to be too small and unsuitable for use as a school. On the 29th of January 1979 all one hundred and forty plus children moved to the newly erected St. Oliver Plunkett School just outside the village and since then the old school has been used as a youth club.

In the early 1930's the Protestant children of the village and the nearby town-lands were taught in a building known as The Johnston Hall. In 1936 they moved to the newly-built Hutton Memorial School, close to the new barracks at the lower end of the village. Just seventy years later this school too was abandoned, when, in 2006, three schools, Dervaghroy, Sixmilecross, and The Hutton Memorial, amalgamated to form The Cooley School, near Sixmilecross.

The old chapel, when first used in the very early 1800s, was but a kind of warehouse. It was renovated or reconstructed on two or three different occasions during the course of almost two centuries. It was toppled and removed when the new church was built in 1984.

For a time, the police (the Royal Irish Constabulary, or RIC) occupied the building that we all knew as the Parochial House. It is now No.37, the home of Cyril Nixon and his family. Records show that the old barracks, near the top end of the village, were built in 1830. Although specifically built for the police, it was not registered as a barracks until 1861. It was vacated in 1936 when a new barracks was built at the lower end of the village. Soon afterwards it was sold for the sum of three hundred pounds. It was then resold and became the home of John Barton and his family until 1974. In that year, when the Barton family decided to move to Omagh, they sold the house in Beragh by public auction. P.J. McClean was the purchaser. He still resides there with his wife and family. It is the only cut-stone building in the village.

The creamery in Beragh was built in the years between 1877 and 1880. Then for over sixty years milk was collected from the many small farmers in a five or six mile radius. Farmers living close by delivered milk to the creamery each morning themselves, while specially designed horse drawn creamery carts collected milk from the outlying farms. Cream was also taken to Beragh creamery from three outlying centres where milk was collected and separated. When separated, the cream was retained and the skim milk returned to the farm. Buttermilk was also available. Both skim milk and buttermilk was fed to calves or pigs. Mr Creighton, who lived across the way, was creamery manager for many years. The creamery closed down in 1942 when Nestlé's factory started up in Omagh. Lorries then collected the milk at the farms or at collection points over a fifteen or twenty mile radius. At this factory all the milk was retained, dried and sold at home or abroad as powdered milk. Nestlé's factory closed down in 2001. Sometime about 1920 the committee of the creamery decided to build a Co-op. with the aim of buying and selling farm produce and other such materials essential for rural dwellers. They chose a site close to the creamery. Stones were carted from old buildings at the Rectory in the townland of Clogherney near the village. When the building commenced and a month or so had expired the creamery manager decided that not enough work was being done to justify the amount of wages being paid. Then after a second warning he sacked the builder and his entire work force.

For quite a while, after the First World War, a recession occurred and as a result many people were left unemployed. It was then that a father and two of his sons, who were finding it difficult to get work, asked to be allowed to finish the job. They were employed and the task was completed in record time. Again there was a drawback. The recession made business and life in general very difficult. A couple of attempts were made to get business going but without success. For a number of years the building was let as a store. It may have been the mid-1930s before a local man, Hubert Caldwell, was employed and he successfully built up a thriving business. As a young man Hubert had 'served his time' with Patton's, a well known business in Monaghan. Hubert bought the Co-op building and the business when the creamery closed down. When he retired in 1957 he sold the property and the stock to the present owner George Weir Gibson. Some time after the Creamery ceased to operate, the committee sold the premises to the members of the Donaghanie Orange Band.

The Northern Bank came to Beragh soon after the First World War, about 1923. The property they bought was a building belonging to Isaac Kidd. I am told that the old house was completely removed and that the new building was erected on the site. Nevertheless, I have no doubt a sizeable amount of money would have passed over the counter in all those years. Mr. Kernan was bank manager in my school days. By sheer coincidence, just this week, customers have been informed that business in the Beragh branch of the Northern Bank will cease on the 1st September 2008.

The Ancient Order of Hibernians (A.O.H) hall was built close to the creamery in the first years of the last century. It was little used until the late Fr. Alfred McKernan bought it for parish use in 1949. In 1954-5 it was extended to more than double its original size. During the next forty years it was used intensively by both young and old. It was here that the youth club, pictures and dances were held and occasional drama and talent shows drew massive crowds. It's sad, but partygoers of today seem to prefer pubs.

# Townsfolk

I believe I could truthfully say that the first day I went to school was but my third time in Beragh village. I had been taken there to be baptised and again to be vaccinated against smallpox. When we were young we were instructed to stay in sight of our home at all times.

Then as the years went by we got to know the occupants of most of the houses and how they earned their living. Sadly, today there are only two or three houses left in the village that are still home to the same family members or their descendants.

Doctor Leitch was an old man who resided in the house across the road from the school. I have good reason to remember him. He lanced a boil on my neck when I was ten years of age and I carry the scar to the present day. Worse still, the operation was not a success. When my mother brought me two weeks later the old doctor had retired and a new doctor, Doctor Watson, had taken over the practice. Shortly after the old doctor's retirement he bought the big house at the corner where the Fintona road leads out. It had previously been a public house, owned by the Clements family. It is now a block of flats.

A very old man, Owen Mullin, owned a house near to the school. My great grandfather's name was Mullin and I am told this old man may have been a relation of our family. His was a dilapidated building and like many more houses at that time it was overrun with rats. The story is told that when Owen made oatmeal porridge for his supper he would leave the small pot down near the dresser to cool. Each evening the rats would fight around the pot and before Owen could take off the lid to get his supper he had to beat them back with the spoon. He lived until he was over ninety.

The next building along was the police barracks. When the police vacated it in the mid-thirties it was then occupied for a number of years by James Barton and his family. James, I think, was an agent for Brown & Noland Books. He also had numerous sidelines. Some paid off, some didn't. During the war years when food was rationed it was necessary to obtain a permit to kill a pig and salt it for one's own use. James applied for and received a permit but slaughtered two pigs. Some time later the police heard about this and paid James a visit (maybe the old barracks had ears). Wth the aid of a vet they 'rebuilt' the pig and found some extras. A few weeks later headings in the local newspapers read, "Beragh man's pig had six legs"

## Characters

*Johnnie Cooke was a cobbler,*
*He would also shave your chin,*
*When he shaved aul' Mick McCullagh*
*His cheeks would not hold in.*
*'White Alec' was a chimney sweep.*
*His face was black with soot.*
*The children often laughed at him*
*But he did not give a hoot.*

Frank Hagan was a tailor,
A good one too at that,
He'd make a suit of clothes for you
All except the hat.
He made a suit for Pat Cleary,
It made him look so thin,
"It's all right breathing out" said Pat,
"But no way can I breathe in"

Myles Canavan was a cooper.
He could make a wooden tub.
Farmers used them often,
'Twas there they mixed pig's grub.
He made staffs for churning
If you cared to have a brash
You had need to be quite careful,
Or you'd cause the cream to splash.

John McCrossan was night watchman,
But he did not sleep one day,
When he nodded off the following night,
The train took the gates away.
Joe Kelly was an old porter
Retired a long time ago,
But he'd carry your attaché-case
Expecting a tip, you know.

Beragh had an old lamplighter
It was his daily toil
To go around each evening
And fill street-lamps with oil
His Christian name was Willie
His surname, I don't know
He was just the old lamplighter
Of long, long, long ago.

*The McGarrity's, they were butchers*
*It was Joe that killed the beast*
*Charlie served out in the shop*
*Where we bought our Sunday feast.*
*Bob McCausland was a diviner*
*'Twas many a spring he found,*
*Then with a pick and a shovel*
*He'd dig deep in the ground.*

*Andy McIvor was a dealer*
*He'd buy the empty bags,*
*He also had a market*
*For iron goods and rags.*
*He had a little pony*
*He fed it well with hay*
*But it had to travel far and fast*
*When it was yoked next day*

A few doors further down the street Patrick McCrystall lived with his wife and young son. At an earlier stage Packie, as he was called, must have acquired some knowledge of the butchery business and later in life neighbours were surprised when they heard that he had decided to open a butchers shop. In those days most butchers slaughtered the animals on their own premises. The garden behind Packie's house stretched down and touched the road that we travelled along when going to the village. Late one evening as my father was coming home he saw a very excited animal galloping down the garden and Packie was in close pursuit. He called for help and my father went to his assistance. Together they managed to get the beast back into a shed. The animal was minus a horn and it had a halter on its head. Packie explained what had happened. It seems that the young assistant whom Packie had employed to help, had let go of the rope and ran for his life just as Packie was about to administer the fatal blow and the animal had escaped minus its horn. The butcher's shop never did materialise.

Many years later Packie's name again made headlines. This time he was working with a pair of horses in a field near the village. The horses were pulling a harrow, which was at least ten-foot wide. For some undisclosed reason Packie left down the reins for a moment. Unfortunately, at the same time, something startled the animals and they bolted. They galloped towards the open gate and managed to get onto the road. As they came close to the village ten or twelve young children were playing in the roadway. Luckily the pounding of the horses' feet and the jingling of the chains alerted them and they all scrambled to safety. The horses, plus the harrow, went out onto the main street and galloped down the footpath. Chips were taken off the steps at the old parochial house and off the bay windows of another house further down the village. No other damage was done and the horses were captured when they slowed down.

Further down at the corner pub we would see the customers, usually four or five oldish men, being ushered out and the shutters going up at nine o'clock each evening. Nine o'clock was closing time and the fact that we had Double Summer time made matters worse. Double Summer time meant that from the month of May until August all clocks were put forward an extra hour. This practice lasted for at least six years. Most people referred to it as 'Mad Time'.

There is also a story told about the old parochial house and a young curate who I can just about remember. It seems he had been in the parish during the time of the death of two parish priests. When a third P.P. was appointed he had major improvements done to the house before he moved in. This included a new stairway, which had two or three bends. During the time that work was in progress no one was allowed in. When the work was completed the new P.P. invited the curate in to give his opinion of the layout. The curate went in the front door, took one look at the stairs and says, "Good gracious, how is anyone expected to get a coffin down them stairs".

Owens's shop did a big grocery and hardware business. Mrs Kathleen Rodgers (nee Owens), wife of Francis Hugh Rodgers, was manager. Francis Hugh was a farmer and was also the local undertaker. He owned the last horse-drawn hearse to be seen in this district. The driver of the horses and hearse on its last journey was James Colton who now resides in Dungannon.

All funerals looked stately in those days. The steady pace of the prancing black horses with their coats brushed and shining, their manes and tails combed and trimmed, and the silver mounted harness polished to perfection all added to the air of dignity. As the hearse moved silently along on rubber shod wheels, the heavy stamping of the two black steeds could be heard above the tread of the mourners. Horses and traps carrying the old or infirm took up the rear as the cortege slowly wound its way along country roads. All shops and business premises along the way and in the village had closed doors and drawn blinds and, as far as possible, the road was kept free of traffic or anything that would inconvenience the cortege. Mickey Conway was gravedigger in those days and it was customary that everyone was buried in his or her own family plot. This meant that bones and skulls were often dug up. If this happened they were carefully placed around the coffin before the grave was closed.

On a lighter note, the story of the McAlister brothers (who were the mill owners) is interesting, especially to those of us who knew them. We were always told that they were the richest people in the district. Be that as it may, we do know that their father bought about ten acres of land on which there was a corn mill, a flax mill and eight or ten mill workers houses. The property was adjacent to Beragh village and the agreed price was £460. The former owner was Henry Watson, and the transaction took place in the month of February 1872. Afterwards a dispute arose about the exact measurement of the property and this became the subject of a high court case in Belfast. A final settlement was reached in June 1873.

The total itemised solicitor's and senior councillor's bill for handling the case was £30-5s-6d. A breakdown of this bill shows:

*Council, 3 contacts @ £2-2s-0d = £6-6s-0d*
*Solicitor, 82 entries on bill varying from one @ £1-0s-0d*
*to £0-0s-6d = £21-9s-6d*
*Stamp on Deed= £2-10s-0d*
*Total = £30-5s-6d*

Today, no one whom we were able to contact can remember the scotch or flax mill working but quite a few remember the corn mill in action and a lesser number of the farming community would have eaten porridge that was made with meal ground at the mill. In the 1930s the mill was in poor condition, sieves were worn and holed, allowing husks and foreign bodies to remain in the meal. This made it quite unpalatable and one local wit was heard to say, "It would take two people spitting for one supping".

Finally, when the water wheel got into a state of disrepair the McAlister brothers decided to buy a Fordson tractor to drive the corn crusher which ground oats or barley for animal meal. The tractor was placed in the house near to the crusher and it worked well when the weather was fine and all doors open. But on a cold wet morning the brothers started up the tractor to grind some oats and neglected to open the doors or windows. Luckily a customer called soon after to collect some meal and on opening the door he found one of the brothers lying on the ground and the other in a distressed state. The fumes of the tractor had overcome them. He managed to get both men out to the fresh air and slowly they both came round. As the one who was lying on the ground opened his eyes and saw the customer he asked, "Do you want it done coarse or fine?"

In 1960 the McAlisters sold the mill and land and retired to a house in the village. On a summer's evening a group of young people were sitting on a seat at a shop door and the discussion was about how much money the McAlisters might have. An older man, the late Bob Lyttle, who was standing nearby spoke up and said, "Listen boys, I don't know how much money the McAlisters might have, and I don't want you to think I have a heap of money in the bank. I try to keep a couple of pounds in it to help to bury me when I cock my toe. But sure when a 'wean'[4] needs a pair of shoes I have to go in and take it out again. I went in yesterday evening to get a couple of pounds and it was the manager himself that was there. He went into yon wee room and came out again empty-handed". He says to me, "Mr Lyttle, I don't want you to think we haven't got your money, but the cashier is off this evening and McAlister's money is sitting on top of yours. When he comes in tomorrow morning I will get him to move it and if you are about at ten o'clock call in and you will get your money".

Davy Smith was a middle-aged man when I was still a young boy. He was a stone mason and many buildings in the neighbourhood bear his trademark. Time of day meant nothing to him. In the summer if the weather was poor Davy could be out on the job before five o'clock if it happened to be a fine morning. To arouse the people of the house where the work was being done he would kick buckets around the yard. He did tidy work but was very hard to attend. "More mort and some small levers" was his constant demand, and when the scaffold was full he might want it changed. Davy built a lot of stone.

There was another man from Clougherney whom I admired very much. He was Mick Mullen, or "Big Mick" as we called him. He was a cousin of my mother and he lived alone in the family abode after his father and mother died. He helped my father for a while when I was small. I suppose that is why he was called Big Mick. If you saw Mick walking in the distance you would think he was slow and lazy but if you walked beside him most likely you would have to run little bits to keep up with him. It was the same at work. Mick made every move count. He owned a few acres among the rocks and kept a couple of cows and their calves. A dozen or so hens and a few turkeys were his entire stock. I forgot about the dog. He had a small terrier dog. It knew his every move and obeyed his every command.

Mick was a skilful hunter. Rabbits were plentiful amongst the rocks but it would not have surprised me in the least if Mick knew just how many there were. If he fancied rabbit for dinner he lifted a short ash plant that always stood at the doorframe and walked towards the rocks, the terrier at his heels.

I ventured with him on one occasion but was politely asked to wait at the gate and he went in to the small field where a number of rabbits were sitting about or grazing. There were big rabbits and small ones, scurrying to the burrows when they saw the dog, but a few crouched down in the grass. Mick walked on, holding the ash plant with the heavy end towards the ground. Then he pointed with the stick in the direction of a rabbit and the dog dashed towards it. Quickly the rabbit sprinted towards the burrow but Mick was well placed. He stooped low and threw the stick in a twirling fashion along the ground, hitting the rabbit's legs and toppling it over, leaving it easy prey for the dog. Mick lifted it up quickly and put it out of misery.

As we strolled back to the house I foolishly mentioned to Mick that he had allowed a bigger rabbit to run past him. He was slow to answer but explained, "That was an 'old she' full of pups". When we got back to the yard Mick fumbled in his waistcoat pocket and took out a penknife and after making a few slits in the rabbit's fur he removed it just like pulling off a sock. Another couple of nicks of the penknife and the rabbit was cleaned out and ready for a wash and the pot.

I never knew Mick to own a greyhound, but a couple of neighbours had a great interest in the hounds and there was always a couple available. Walking the dogs or going hunting was our way of spending a Sunday evening. Usually we would meet and then decide where to go but on one occasion it was arranged that we would start early and go to the coal hill the following week.

Now, it was well known that on this bog or hill there was a hare that was often chased but was never caught. In fact we heard it said that if it got too far in front, it would stop and wait for the dogs.

Big Mick always referred to this hare as 'the lady'. Who knows, maybe there were more hares than one. Anyway, as arranged, we had just gathered on Sunday afternoon and were ready to set off when a small van pulled up beside us and two young fellows got out. One of them opened the back of the van and out jumped two big greyhounds. No one spoke; Mick gave an accusing look around the group and turned for home.

He did not go too far until he stopped for a moment. He turned round and walked past us without speaking. We followed in silence and when we reached the hill we fanned out. We had not gone far until the hare arose and the two local dogs gave chase. Then the two strange dogs followed and were catching up rapidly. Soon the leading dog was close to the hare and to a novice hunter like myself it looked like a quick kill. But not so, a sharp turn to the right and the hare gained a few yards but these yards were quickly eaten up and another turn was needed. Now the hare was coming back towards us. I glanced in Mick's direction and saw him change the stick in his hand. Surely Mick wouldn't, I thought, the poor hare deserved a chance. But then he bent down and the stick went twirling. I couldn't watch. I looked away but as I did, I heard a loud yelp. I looked back and saw the leading greyhound topple over in the path of the second dog and both were rolling on the ground. The hare was now almost out of sight and travelling at its normal speed. The two young men rushed over, howling abuse at Mick but he walked at his usual pace, lifted his stick and in his normal quiet voice said, "I missed". I doubt if he did.

On the thirtieth of June 2005 the Hutton Memorial School in Beragh closed for the last time as the children dispersed for their summer holidays. It was erected in the mid-1930s and named in honour of the late Master John Hutton B.A. who, for many years, had taught the children in the Johnston Memorial Hall. He was a learned man who had gained a gold medal in the Advanced Course in 1900 and who was one of the most accomplished teachers under the Board of National Education. He became involved in the Total Abstinence Movement and during the years 1911 and 1912 he delivered 50 admirable lectures in the Clogher, Omagh, and Strabane districts.

At that time numerous pledges were said to have been taken. As a retiree Master Hutton spent much of his time giving extra lessons to young people of all creeds who wished to improve their knowledge or learn an extra subject. His brown 'Riley 9' car with yellow spoked wheels was one of the first cars in the village.

The first houses in Beragh village, we are told, were built over two hundred years ago. Entries between houses were narrow and suitable only for horses and carts. Robert John Clarke had a garage in his yard where he worked at bicycles. Later he bought a car with the intention of starting a taxi business. When the car was delivered the driver carefully manoeuvred it into Clarke's yard. All seemed fine until the first customer arrived requiring a lift, and Robert John, try as he might was unable to get the car out of the yard. The driver who delivered the car was called but he too failed. Not until part of the wall was taken away could the car be got out of the yard.

Another man who deserves a mention was old William Hackett. He was elderly and retired before I knew him. His house was mid-way up the village and it had no back door as it was next to the entry. In the summer time we often saw him carrying food for the fowl that he reared down in his garden. Then later on in the year he would one day emerge from the garden followed by six or seven, almost fully grown geese, waddling in single file as he led them to the river at the lower end of the village. Here he stood on the bank as they swam and splashed for a time in the water. What signal he gave them we never did find out, but as soon as he turned towards home, the geese left the water and followed him single file back up the village, a distance of about four hundred yards.

Being born and reared in the Beragh area, which has a mixed community, we were taught to understand that although some neighbours had different political and religious views than ours, they were still good people and entitled to their opinion. The Fentons were one such family who lived close at hand and we encountered them most days as we went to and came from school or the village. They were about the same age group as my father and were good neighbours. One of the family had fought in the First World War. I think he survived the war but died of natural causes years later.

Bob was the eldest one I knew. He was a builder, or tradesman, as such men were called at that time. I remember him helping to remove the old thatch and put a new slated roof on our home in Laragh in 1934 or '35. Years later I picked up a few tricks of the trade from him as he built or repaired some of the farm buildings. He was a married man and had his own home and family. His sister Annie lived in England. I understand she was a schoolteacher. His other siblings, Willie, Joe and Minnie, still resided in the homestead. They owned a lot of land; three or four farms, and employed two fulltime workmen.

Willie was the boss. He was also the horseman, working with a team of horses, ploughing, harrowing, reaping crops or digging the potatoes. They had a spare horse with which one of the workmen did the carting and other odd jobs. Minnie was the housekeeper. Their home was relatively new, being built in the late twenties. Joe attended the cattle, helped with the milking and kept the place tidy. He was a weekly visitor or 'céilíer' at our house in the winter nights. He had a different céilí house for each night of the week and always had wonderful tales to tell. Tales of the fairs and the cattle and the prices, but he really excelled when horses were mentioned. I can remember him describing horses that he saw in the fair to my father, whom he always called Paddy.

"By the high and low Paddy, yon horse stands a good eighteen hands high, with a good sweet head and a white face. He has four white legs and a foot as big as a plate. He has a good back and a wide front. Do you know, Paddy, you could wheel the turf barrow between his front legs. Kelly sold him to a wee lame man from the 'Brae Face' for forty five quid. Do you know, Paddy, if there's not a hole as big as your head in yon horse, he's dirt cheap". Joe often used words and names that my mother bade us not to repeat except in our prayers.

Willie was a different sort of person. As I said he worked with the team of horses but he expected the workmen to have the horses feed in the manger at evening time. Most evenings Willie visited the pub but as nine o'clock was closing time he seldom overindulged. In the morning he arose early, fed the horses and washed enough potatoes to fill the boiler and then, as he said himself, he 'footered about'[5] until the breakfast was ready.

Occasionally in the hay or harvest time, if the weather was poor Willie might visit the pub early in the day and on such an occasion he might be glad of a shoulder to lean on as he staggered home. I remember one time, I think it might have been during the war years and on a day near to July the twelfth, my father was coming from the village when he saw Willie lying in a not too comfortable position close to the hedge on the grass verge. He got off his bicycle and was assisting him to get back on his feet when Willie made a reference to the Pope, which hit a raw nerve with my father. Without further ado he left Willie where he found him and came home. As we were taking our tea my mother seemed to become aware that something was amiss with my father and enquired what was wrong. When he told her she too got worried and intoned, "If anything happens to the aul' cratur[6] we'll never forgive ourselves", whereupon my father got on his bicycle, went back, and helped Willie home. The event was never mentioned again. Willie and Joe helped when the steamroller came and we gave them a hand at the harvest and the potato gathering.

I had never met Annie at this time but I heard neighbours talking about her being unwell over in England. Willie had gone over to see her. When he returned he confirmed that she was very poorly and shortly afterwards word came that she wanted to come home. Again Willie went to help her on the journey. A couple of days later I was in the cart with my father when we met Willie and enquired how Annie was. "I never seen the like of her" says Willie. "I had to carry her onto the boat and I could hardly find the weight of her in my arms. There is not wan[7] pick on her! My goodness, you could drop her down the hole in a straw".

But Annie survived. She regained her health but never put on any weight. Years after, she attended a poultry meeting in the Johnston Memorial Hall. She arrived rather late and as the seats were all taken she sat on a window sill. A cup of tea was being served later but at that stage Annie could not be found. A young girl who was helping with the tea noticed that the blind on the window where Annie was sitting had gone up. She looked at it for a moment and asked, "Do you think has she snapped up with the blind?"

It's hard to believe, but it is a fact that seventy years ago there was not a farm tractor in this district or even in a much wider area. In those days when we spoke of horsepower we really meant horse power. On the larger farms it was necessary to have three or sometimes four farm horses and often a pony or a light-boned horse which was kept for driving on the road in a trap or light spring cart. It was used when travelling to fairs or markets or more often when going shopping. On Sundays it took the family in style to their place of worship. Bread carts, were drawn by horses, as were grocery carts or "tea carts", to give them the title they were more commonly known by. Medium-sized farms required two horses and most small farms had one. The latter mostly worked in partnership with a near neighbour's horse when a "team" (two horses) was required to do a job.

As all horses required to be shod quite often, the making and fitting of horseshoes on each animal was work for highly skilled blacksmiths and in this trade none surpassed the skill of the late Mick McMackin. After Mick had served his time to the blacksmith's trade, he came to Beragh village and plied his trade in the yard behind his house. Later he managed to buy six or seven acres of land at the end of the village and on this he built his home and a forge and here he was happy to toil and rear his family. In the early spring when all the horses were being got ready for the busy season, the blacksmith had a hectic time. At the height of his career Mick McMackin was known to make and fit shoes on eight horses in one long day's work. At the times when there were no horses in the forge, there were always a variety of tools and implements waiting to be made or mended. Putting iron hoops or bands on cartwheels was a job that required great skill and a very big turf fire. To do this job it was necessary to build a big fire all the way around the iron hoops and keep it burning until the entire iron hoop was red hot. This fire was lit outside the forge.

One day as Mick was putting hoops on wheels, he had a great fire blazing when the local curate happened to come along. He stopped and spoke to Mick. "That is surely a great fire you have going".

"Do you know Father," says Mick, "if the aul' devil was standing in the middle of that fire, he would get his death of cold!"

Mick had a great sense of humour. I remember, as a young boy, being sent to the forge to collect some small tool that was being repaired and Mick said to me, "I hear your father has bought a new horse". I assured him that was correct. "He must be very small," said he. I argued that the horse was not small. "Well someone told me," said Mick "that your father had to put a knot on his tail to keep him from jumping through the collar".

Although Mick smiled and joked he must have been an ill man. On the advice of his doctor he agreed to go to a hospital in Belfast for an operation. On the morning of the day that he went into hospital he arose early and shod two horses before he left. Later, as he walked down the village to the railway station accompanied by his son, he stopped and went back to give someone a couple of shillings he thought he owed, and then off he went on the train. Another son who worked in Belfast met him at the station and accompanied him to the hospital. The next day he was to pass away on the operating table. When the news of his death reached Beragh, everyone was stunned. Years later his home and forge were taken away to accommodate road works, but memories of Mick will never fade in the hearts and minds of those who knew him.

# Races

Easter Monday was a very special day back in the year 1940 and for many years before. It was on this day every year that the horse races were held at Dervaghroy. When I speak of, or write about horse racing I don't mean children on ponies, or even a local derby, I mean horse racing big time, on a course probably as long, and definitely as heavy, as the Grand National. It did not have as many jumps but they were over real fences and just as dangerous.

I only managed to get there once. In 1939 I cried and had begged to be allowed to go but my pleading was in vain. I was told I could go when I was big enough to hang the horse's collar up on its special wooden peg. I managed it in 1940. The late Peter Kelly took me there on the bar of his bike. I was small in the crowd and saw little of the horses. But then, who wants to look at horses when there was so much more to be seen.

Race-goers were there from near and far, from all over Ireland and even from England and Scotland. Some came by train to Beragh or Omagh railway stations and were taxied out to the course. Others got there by bus. Great numbers came in automobiles of all shapes and sizes with massive headlamps, wide running boards, loads of shining chrome and some with collapsible tops. They came in their hundreds on their bikes and many walked for miles. There were gentry in top hats and swallow-tailed coats, and ladies in mink furs and Easter bonnets. Even some locals dared to don their "plus fours" and wax their handlebar moustaches. I had never before seen such a gathering of toffs in my life. At that time both my grand mothers were still wearing black shawls. The horses too had strange names, compared to our horse which was called Prince.

A long row of noisy bookies, surrounded by bags and buckets of money, scanned the crowd for prospective customers as they skilfully kept watch for a change of odds on the other bookies' blackboards. One particular bookmaker had a row of £5 and £10 notes secured to the silk band around his great big hat.

Another one was a man I knew. His name was Sam McGee. I remember him on different occasions calling at our house looking for old hens. On his first visits he came on a bicycle that had a sack tied to the bar into which he put the fowl. On later calls he had acquired a small pony and trap. On the day of the races, here he was, dressed in a swallow-tail coat and top hat, standing knee-deep in money and expertly filling the role of a confident bookie.

I had been given a two shilling piece coin (a florin) before I left home, with instructions not to lose it. I held it tightly in my hand in my trouser pocket. I think it was in the second race that a horse fell and was killed at the third jump. His name was Red Sails and quite a few people had placed their bets on him. A glance at the map of the area where the races took place might be of interest to some. I am indebted to Samuel Mc Dowell, whose farm adjoins the lands over which the races were run, for helping to map out the course, the jumps, the car parks, etc.

One thing it does not immediately point out though is the class distinction that was commonplace at the time. Notice how there were two car parks; one, which was some distance from the assembly field, charged a parking fee of five shillings, while the other one for the upper classes had a fee of ten shillings. More apparent were the catering and toilet facilities. While ample accommodation was made available for the crowd in general, special arrangement was made for the gentry. A temporary bridge, or a "kesh" as it was called at that time, was fitted over the small stream that divides the townlands of Dervaghroy and Raw. This "flyover", which was discreetly guarded, led to more hygienic conveniences for the elite.

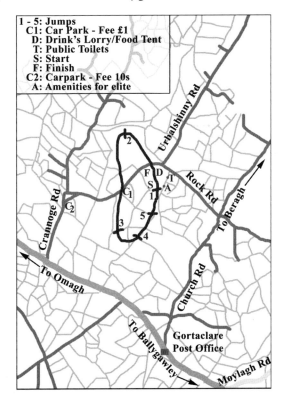

1 - 5: Jumps
C1: Car Park - Fee £1
D: Drink's Lorry/Food Tent
T: Public Toilets
S: Start
F: Finish
C2: Carpark - Fee 10s
A: Amenities for elite

He also had another interesting bit of information and was willing to supply a relic to confirm his story. It seems that Jas McAllister & Sons, Ballymena were the main supplier of drinks at the last race meeting in 1940. A lorry from the firm drove into a field where a temporary bar had been erected adjacent to the racecourse.

All went well until the event was over and the lorry was reloaded for the return journey. Because of the soft ground the driver had difficulty in turning the lorry and as a result the steering broke. In those early days of motorised transport it took quite a long time to get a spare part for a vehicle and as the lorry could not be moved the unsold beer, spirits, and soft drinks were carried into a barn-loft at the nearby farmyard owned by the McDowell family. Few, if any, of the neighbours knew the drinks were there but an old man of the road sometimes slept in the barn as he made his way from house to house. He happened to call in late on this particular night and must have thought he had arrived in paradise! It was a couple of days before he was discovered and the most of a week before he was able to resume his travels. When the lorry was repaired and being reloaded, a couple of crates of stout were given to the McDowell family and a few bottles still remain unopened sixty-seven years later.

Thanks to the internet, and the local press, we are able to give an accurate (though shortened) report on the last meeting:

*Seskinore Harriers*
*Most Successful Race Meeting in History of Club*

*The annual race meeting under the auspices of the Seskinore Harriers, which was held on Easter Monday over the splendid race course at Dervaghroy, so kindly granted by Mr. John D. Watson, was the most successful in the history of the Club. It attracted huge crowds of race enthusiasts from all over the country. It was an exceedingly popular event and was favoured with the most delightful weather conditions.*

*The course was in excellent shape and the Harriers are under a deep debt of obligation to Mr. Watson, who not only grants the use of the course absolutely free but also goes to infinite trouble in preparation of same. Since the races have been transferred to Mr. Watson's course they have become more popular and may soon rival such big fixtures as the Maze and Ballyhaft.*

*On the day, there were five races:*

*Race 1: The Welter Race for horses the property since January 1st of subscribers contributing to any hunt in Ireland, or of farmers over whose lands the Seskinore Harriers hunt.*
*Distance three miles. Weight, 13 stone.*
*Winner: Baile-mhic-a-adhoe (Mr. W.B. Smyth)*

*Race 2: Governor's Cup, with £5 added.*
*Weight 12 stone.*
*Winner: Swinstep (Mr. R. Moore)*

*Race 3: Novice Race. (Open)*
*For horses which have never won a point-to-point race of any description, the property since January 1st.1939, of subscribers*

*to any hunt in Ireland, or of farmers over whose land the*
*Seskinore Harriers hunt.*
*Weight, 12 stone 7lbs.*
*Winner: Crafty Prince (Mr. T. Cooke)*

**Race 4:** *Ladies' Race (Open)*
*Weight, 12 stone 7 lbs.*
*Winner: Take Me (Mr. G. Taylor)*

**Race 5:** *Seskinore Cup.*
*For horses the property since December 15th.1938, of members*
*of Seskinore Harriers or of farmers over whose land the hounds*
*hunt and have been hunted at least eight times during the*
*season 1938/ 1939*
*Weight 12 stone 7lbs.*
*Winner: May Flower (Miss.J. Warmock).*

# War Time

On many occasions in the year 1938 and until we got our summer holidays in 1939, our teacher, Mr Conway, often told us of the continual threat of an outbreak of war. He told us how Hitler insisted that all German children be rigorously drilled in Nazism and any parents who failed to comply had their children taken away and placed in a state school. On the big map of Europe which hung on the wall in our school the teacher pointed out how, on the 14th of March 1938, the German army had marched into Austria.

September the 3rd was a beautiful harvest day. We had just cut the last swathe of corn of the harvest in a neighbour's field when the woman of the house brought out our evening tea. She told us that war had been declared. Already enemy fighter planes were over cities and towns in England and Scotland and air duels were taking place. Two or three of our group of harvesters, as well as myself, were still young teenagers, country teenagers, who knew little about big towns or cities. At school we had been told a lot about how war would affect all of us. But, if tomorrow was to be a fine day, and it looked promising, we would be starting to stack the corn. That meant rides in the cart and building loads of sheaves. The only cloud on our horizon was that in a few days the holidays would be over and for us it was back to school for another year or so. Little did we know that, slowly but surely, unimaginable changes were to take place in our lifetime.

On October 5th 1939, as the war intensified, the German Army entered Czechoslovakia. Britain's response was to conscript 250,000 more men, of which 158,000 were sent to France together with 25,000 vehicles.

Food rationing was announced in early December and came into force on January 8th. Rationing, along with the blackouts, were the aspects of war that had the greatest impact on our daily lives. Weekly allowances were as follows: Butter 4 ounces; Bacon and Ham, 4 ounces; Sugar, 12 ounces. Later food rationing was extended to meat, and this came into force in March 1940. It was rationed on the basis of value, each person's weekly allowance being one shilling and two pennies worth. Offal, rabbit, poultry, game and fish did not require coupons at that time; nor did brawn, sausages, pies or paste.

The New Emergency Powers Act gave the Government the power to impose a 100 per cent tax on profits, and practically unlimited authority over every person, and all property and land. As the war progressed, the restrictions imposed became increasingly severe and affected the most basic aspects of everyone's lifestyle. For example, women were asked to conserve wood by wearing flat heels and the buying and selling of all new cars was banned. However there was welcome relief in December of 1940 when the Food Minister announced extra rations for Christmas; each person was allowed four ounces of sugar and two ounces of tea.

On January 26th 1942 several thousand soldiers of the U.S. Army land in Northern Ireland. A large contingent of these troops was billeted locally in Seskinore Forest. It was amazing to see how they camouflaged their presence in among the trees.

By February of that year even the water was rationed! People were asked to take fewer baths with no more than five inches of warm water. Plimsoll lines were painted on public and hotel baths. Soap was rationed to one tablet per month. Shaving soap was not rationed but was difficult to obtain and razor blades were also very short in supply. Men were asked to re-sharpen their old blades by rubbing them around the inside of a tumbler. Good advice if one could lay their hands on a tumbler, they were less plentiful than the blades! Restrictions on clothing were also imposed. No double-breasted suits or coats, no buttons on sleeves and no turn-ups on trousers were permitted. Ladies wear was likewise restricted. Styles were to be limited, no frills, shorter skirts, bare legs and no embroidery on underwear or nightwear. By July even the simple pleasures in life were curtailed when sweets were rationed and driving for pleasure was banned. Even icing on cakes was forbidden! Cardboard wedding cakes with 'icing' made of chalk were being offered for rent by confectioners and hotels in lieu of the real thing. It may be of interest to some readers to see the World War II Rationing Timeline below:

**1939 World War II declared**

| | |
|---|---|
| 1939 | – Petrol rationed |
| 8 January 1940 | – Bacon, butter and sugar rationed |
| 11 March 1940 | – All meat rationed |
| July 1940 | – Tea and margarine rationed |
| March 1941 | – Jam rationed |
| May 1941 | – Cheese rationed |
| 1 June 1941 | – Clothing rationed and coupons issued |
| June 1941 | – Eggs rationed |
| July 1941 | – Coal rationed |
| January 1942 | – Rice and dried fruit rationed |
| February 1942 | – Soap, tinned tomatoes and peas rationed |
| March 1942 | – Gas and electricity rationed |
| 26 July 1942 | – Sweets and chocolate rationed |
| August 1942 | – Biscuits rationed |
| 1943 | – Sausages rationed |

**1945 World War II Ends**

| | |
|---|---|
| 25 July 1948 | – End of flour rationing |
| 15 March 1949 | – End of clothes rationing |
| 19 May 1950 | – End of rationing for canned and dried fruit, chocolate biscuits, treacle, syrup, jellies and mincemeat. |
| September 1950 | – End of rationing for soap |
| 3 October 1952 | – End of tea rationing |
| 1953 | – End of sweet and sugar rationing |
| 4 July 1954 | – All food rationing ends. |

But the rationing was only one aspect of the daily effects of the war on the local community. Every man, woman, and child received an identity card, a gas mask, and a ration book. A complete blackout was imposed and within a few days shops were sold out of black curtain material. Few people owned cars in this district, but all night drivers were required to manage using just one headlight. This light was to be covered with cardboard or such material, and, with only a 2-inch hole to allow some little light filter through. Cyclists were also required to have all lights shielded. Even the interior lights on buses were to be left unlit unless the windows were fitted with proper blinds. This caused problems, especially for the conductors and elderly passengers alike. Young people took it in their stride; some even turned it to their advantage.

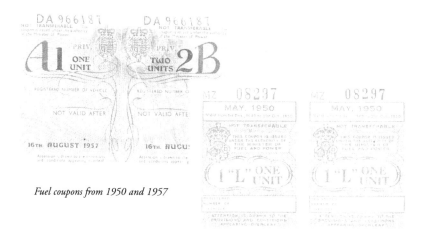

*Fuel coupons from 1950 and 1957*

Few people today could imagine what complete darkness is really like. On cloudy, moonless nights it was well nigh impossible to find one's way, even on well-trodden paths. One could usually manage on the roadway by walking close to the grass verge but seventy years ago when people went visiting at night-time they often used short cuts through the fields. Some great stories were told of mishaps that occurred during the blackout years. I have no doubt that most were true but one or two seemed more like fiction.

I know a lady, she still lives nearby, who on her way home from the village one dark night fell on top of a donkey as it lay in the centre of the road. The terrified girl received a couple of minor injuries as both struggled to get back on their feet.

Another young lady from the village had a boyfriend who got the loan of his father's car, in which he would call to collect her every Wednesday night. He always parked in the same spot and the young lass immediately dashed out and quickly got into the passenger seat. On one particularly dark night as the girl waited by the window a car pulled up at the spot. Without hesitation she ran to the car, opened the front passenger door and hopped in, only to find herself on the knee of the local curate whom a taxi driver was dropping off after being out on a call. She may have said sorry, but she definitely did not wait for a blessing. Her 'date' called later. This time she made a more dignified approach!

While that young lady may have been temporarily embarrassed, Cupid was labelled with aiding and abetting in a prank which had a more permanent effect on the love life of a man, we will call him Ned. We are told that for a number of years, Ned was friendly with, and a regular visitor to the home of a spinster lady who was known locally as Miss Kelly. Neighbours talked a lot about romance but it did not seem to blossom. Then, early in the war years a girl called Peggy, who was a niece of the lady, came to work in a shop in the village. During the week the young lady was to board with her aunt but went home at weekends. It wasn't long until neighbours noticed that Ned's visits became more frequent, that he shaved more often, took off his hobnail boots and put on his Sunday shoes when he went to visit. A local wit was heard to comment that Ned was now courting the cat for the kitten.

As autumn merged into winter and the evenings darkened, Ned was always ready and waiting at the shop door to chaperone the young lady to her digs. This arrangement continued until one evening just before Christmas, and, as the couple came close to the house, Ned plucked up courage, put his arm around Peggy and asked her to marry him. Although Peggy showed great surprise she didn't say no. She told him that she was going home for Christmas but she would be back on Boxing Day. She asked him to wait at the wee turf shed at the gable of the house at nine o'clock on that evening and promised that he would get a definite answer then. She then gave him a quick peck on the cheek, wished him a Happy Christmas and skipped into the house.

Ned was so sure that his proposal was accepted and his first task next day was to visit the jewellers to purchase a ring. Over the following couple of days his appetite was poor and he could feel his heart thump but on Boxing Day he got ready early and was at the turf shed long before the allotted time.

It was a moonless night, dark and cold, but sure enough on the stroke of nine he saw the flash of light as the door opened and a female figure emerged. As she made her way towards him in the darkness Ned went to meet her and threw his arms round her. She buried her head against his shoulder but said nothing. Now, feeling very confident, he bent his head and whispered "Peggy will you marry me?" Without hesitation came the answer. "Yes, I'll marry you Ned. Sure I thought you'd never ask". Quickly she lifted her head, gave him a great big kiss and again shyly laid her head on his shoulder. Fumbling in his waistcoat pocket he produced the engagement ring and with a shaking hand he managed to put it on her finger. This earned him another smothering kiss in the pitch darkness. Still clinging to each other they ventured to the door and the shelter of the house. Now, for the past few days Ned had ample time to study and rehearse for this moment, but no power on earth would have prepared him for the sight that was about to confront him. As he opened the door and stepped back to allow his fiancée to enter, the colour drained from his face, and his knees almost gave way as the reality of the situation dawned on him. For there, sitting in a comfortable chair by a cosy fire was a complete stranger and on his knee, looking a little sheepish but quite happy was young Peggy. Only then did he remember that the older lady's name was also Peggy. Even before he could make up his mind whether to take to his heels and disappear, or stand his ground and make the best of a most embarrassing situation, the two 'brides-to-be' were comparing engagement rings. Eventually he stepped inside and closed the door. It was clear he could run, but equally clear that he could not hide. Even before he had made his way to the fireside, Aunt Peggy stepped close to him and put her arm around him. She then invited her niece and her fiancé to join them in the parlour, where another fire blazed in the grate and on the table was a lavish meal for four.

The late Joe Fenton, who was a regular céilíer at our home, told a great story about the blackout. He arrived one night with a lot of scratches on his head, his face and on his hands. When asked what had befallen him he explained, in a colourful manner, how he had been making his way home the previous night and it was extremely dark. As he was coming through the fields he was obliged to keep close to the fence which acted as a guide. Even though he moved with great care he managed to trip on something soft and whatever it was seemed to come up to meet him as he fell. He said "I landed fair on its back and away it went, at a gallop. By the high and low Paddy, I would have sworn that the devil had run away with me. My hat fell off and the next thing the brute did was to go straight through the thorn hedge. Jimenty japers, Paddy, I was sure my two lugs were torn off. It took me half-ways through a thick hedge and when I got stuck it went on and left me hanging on the thorns. I thought I was going to be stuck there all night. It took me half an hour to get back on my feet and my old coat was torn to ribbons".

Joe was a pitiful looking sight. It was discovered afterwards that the brute that had carried him away was his own big black-faced ram!

## War and Peace

Whenever there's mention of the war in Iraq,
We elderly people were inclined to look back,
Over sixty-four years to nineteen thirty nine
When world war broke out and the weather was fine.
We were cutting the corn on that very same day,
When big Katy Curley came out with our tay.
The bread-man had called and gave her the news,
A strong hefty fellow was young Danny Hughes.

We were young at the time; it didn't bother us much,
There was no television to keep us in touch.
That wasn't the way our young lives were fashioned,
But we got a surprise when the sugar was rationed.
So too was the bacon and butter in turn,
But we salted a pig and had milk in the churn.
Then after a while it was classed as a crime,
You'd be summoned if caught with a pig in the brine.

Bananas and oranges were not on display,
And by Jove it was bad when they rationed the tay.
Sultanas and raisins were not offered for sale,
If you asked for grapes you just heard a sad tale.
You could only buy sweets if you had a token,
'Twas easy those years to keep lent unbroken.
Equipment was scarce if you liked to go sporting,
And chocolate was kept for the nights we went courting.

Ladies silk stockings could no longer be seen,
They just used a dark pencil to draw the back seam.
Coupons were issued for every stitch that we wore,
You would be in some pickle if your trousers got tore.
We were issued with gas masks, there's still some about,
Life wouldn't be pleasant with yon thing on your snout.

Computers weren't heard of, and a mouse was a mouse.
Asbestos was used for the roof of the house.

Petrol was rationed, if you had a car,
With the wee drop you got, you would not go far,
If your journey was necessary you applied for a pass
Frank Owens was fined pounds for driving to Mass.
But still we were happy and safe from all harm,
Around a turf fire all cosy and warm
With the song of the crickets and the kettle boiled hot,
And the tay sitting drawing in the big black teapot

*Fuel coupons 1950*

*Beragh railway station*

# The Great Northern Railway

The strange thing about Beragh Railway Station was that it was not actually located in Beragh. Both the railway and the railway station were across the Cloughfin River in the townland of Cooley. We are extremely grateful to a young Omagh lady, Miss Susan McNamee, for her help in providing us with an abundance of information about the Great Northern Railway. Her thesis, The Birth of the Great Northern Railway in Tyrone, provided us with oodles of data about the railways which was hitherto obscure.

We learned that the first railway in Britain ran from Liverpool to Manchester. It opened in 1830. Four years later the railway made its debut in Ireland. Back then there were many debates, discursions, disagreements, and objections, even court cases, about which routes the lines should take.

For a start, most railways originated from the ports, like Dublin, Cork, Belfast and Derry. We understand the first two lines in the North were from Belfast to Portadown and from Derry to Enniskillen via Strabane and Omagh. The line reached Enniskillen on 19th of August 1854.

The line from Portadown, via Dungannon, Pomeroy, Carrickmore, Sixmilecross and Beragh, reached Omagh in 1861. It had been built in stages. It figures out that my great-grandparents would have been in their prime in those days. I understand that my great-grandfather did ride on the train. The story is told of how he boarded the train at Omagh, probably fell asleep and missed getting off in Beragh. He landed in Sixmilecross where he raised a row. He claimed the train did not stop and the fact that others had got off would not even convince him. His comment was "She blew but she never stopped". To prevent a major row developing a neighbour who happened to come on the scene got him into his horse's trap and left him at Beragh station. I understand he wasn't a tee-totaller.

It is sad to think that there is not one mile of railway track in use in the county of Tyrone at the present time. It is sad too to think of the number of local men who lost their jobs when the railway closed down. Gangs of men worked together changing sleepers and rails and kept the track in perfect condition. Others continually walked along the track, using a sledgehammer to ensure that all wedges were tightly in place. Some inspected bridges and culverts in case lodgements of water damaged embankments.

**ALL STEAMED UP**
William Dixon was station-master in Beragh, Co. Tyrone between the wars. His daughter-in-law, Mrs Dixon of Belfast, tells us the steam train was a great way of carrying large numbers to the seaside resorts.

Every station had a station master, a signalman, a ticket seller and a number of porters. In early days all the staff were expected to take great pride in their station and there were regular inspections, even prizes for the best kept station. A new beginner's first job was to see that the toilets and waiting rooms were kept clean and that fires were lit in the signal box, the station master's office and in the waiting rooms. The goods store was also to be kept tidy.

The porters helped when wagons were being shunted into the sidings or goods sheds. They used long iron bars to attach or undo the great heavy links of chain that coupled the wagons or carriages to the engines. This was a dangerous operation which required split-second timing in conjunction with the engine driver and the guardsman shunting and braking the train. The porters also helped to load or unload the goods and animals onto or from the wagons.

I remember a yarn that was told about an old station master who was in charge at Beragh a long time ago. His name was Finnegan. It seems his superiors had criticized him for sending in a very lengthy and detailed report regarding the derailing of a wagon at a faulty spot in the goods yard. Two days later a second wagon became derailed. His report this time read as follows. Wagon, in again, off again, on again, out again, Finnegan.

All supplies for the shops in the village, and indeed for the many country shops, arrived at the railway station. Some shop owners had their own horses and carts while others had to pay to get their goods delivered. In Sixmilecross the late John Duffy had a steady job carting goods from the station with his donkey and cart. He was even known to do the ten mile (each way) journey to Omagh to collect supplies.

In the summer time, large blocks of dry ice, used when making ice-cream, would arrive at the station. If one was lucky, the shop owner, Mrs. Fyffe, who made and sold the ice cream, might ask to have a block taken up the village on a railway barrow. The pay for this job was a great big cone of lovely ice cream.

Trains ran on this local stretch of line several times each day. Although we seldom had reason to travel on them, we had a use for them. They were our timepieces. Very few people in my early working days had the luxury of a watch. Many depended on the trains as their timetable.

We all knew the "quarter to nine". We were supposed to have our morning chores completed, our breakfast finished and be working in the field when it came up the line. A heavy goods train might rattle by after that but we knew the noise of the "half eleven". We were supposed to work on for about twenty minutes and then go in for our dinner. Dinner was usually ready just after twelve and we would have a rest as the horses were allowed an hour to feed. Most days our evening tea was brought out to the field where we were working and, as a rule, we would just have it taken and would get to our feet when the "half four" would make its way towards Omagh. In later years, what was known as the "rail bus" or rail car replaced this train.

For gentlemen farmers and their labourers the mail train, at half five signalled the end of work in the fields for the day. They returned to the yard to do the milking and the evening chores. In our case some one person was dispatched to help with the milking and all others continued working until around seven o'clock. Indeed, in the hay or harvest time, if the weather was fine it often happened that a second helping of tea was sent out and then work would continue until the light faded and the dew fell.

While business people did make use of the trains to travel and carry their goods, and some workers and secondary school children found it convenient, most country people were seldom on the trains. In fact I've known a few who were never on a train. Having said that, the Sunday evening excursion train to Bundoran attracted crowds. The fare was 2s/ 6d (half a crown) or about 12 pennies in our present day money.

In the war years and into the late 1940s, this excursion train continued to run to the seaside all through the winter. It was then known as "the sugar train". Every Sunday evening the engine and four or five carriages full of small-time smugglers made their way to the seaside town. For the most part the customs officers seemed to turn a blind eye in its direction, but on a couple of occasions they pounced. I only ventured on the trip on two occasions. The first trip was uneventful. The second proved to be more exciting. It must have been about 1946 or 1947 and near to Christmas time. Sugar was in short supply at our house. I was given enough money to cover my train fare and to buy two stone of sugar. I got an extra couple of shillings so that I could get a cup of tea.

It didn't turn out to be much fun. It was necessary to buy the sugar as soon as we arrived in case the supply ran out. Then, having made the purchase it was essential to guard it until it was time to make the return journey. Bundoran, in mid-winter on a wet Sunday evening wasn't a pleasant place to be away back over sixty years ago, and I didn't happen to meet anyone I knew well until I returned to the train for the return journey.

To make matters worse, passengers weren't made welcome back to the station until it was almost time to make the homeward journey. Then, when we were all aboard and waiting for the train to pull out, we were told that the customs officials had arrived and were searching the train. Sure enough, they started at the front and were working their way down through the carriages. Two men on the platform had a huge, four-wheeled trolley on which they packed the bags of sugar that the officials inside the carriages handed out through the open windows.

The message filtered down through the train that each person was being allowed to keep two pounds of sugar. All the rest was being confiscated. I knew for certain that I was going to lose my sugar. I was sitting by the window in the side of the carriage furthest from the platform and, knowing I was going to lose the sugar, I let down the window and hung the two bags on the door handle outside and pulled up the window. As I did this a few of the passengers watched but no one said a word.

Frank Donnelly, a man from the Beragh district whom I knew very well, happened to be in the same compartment and we chatted for a second. When the "raiders" entered the carriage we were in, everyone who was carrying sugar was allowed to keep two pounds and all the rest was handed out the window. When I was asked I'm afraid I told a white lie. I claimed to be with the other Beragh man and no further questions were asked. I waited until the train had pulled out before I opened the window and sure enough the sugar was there, safe and sound. I gave my partner in crime a couple of pounds of sugar for backing my story. He is still alive and well and I was talking to him only a short time ago.


## The Sugar Train

During the war years times weren't good,
We required coupons to buy our food,
Ones ration of sugar was ever so small,
And there was days when we had none at all.

But the good old sugar train ran up and down,
Starting off from the station at Portadown,
It carried us safely to Bundoran strand,
Where waves splashed out on golden sand.

But it was not the strand we went to see,
But to buy some sugar to put on our tea,
Those who craved for the smoke of a cigarette
Would purchase as many as they could get.

*And for the man who smoked a pipe*
*A bar of tobacco of any type.*
*Back in those days most women could bake,*
*So we'd bring home some fruit for the Christmas cake.*

*Now its sixty years ago since that train ran down the track,*
*It stirs up many memories when our minds just wander back.*
*Memories of the things we did but can never do again,*
*Like travelling to Bundoran on the good old Sugar Train.*

Salesmen and company representatives would arrive at the station. Dressed in a black swallow-tailed coat and pinstriped trouser they would hire a taxi to take them to a hotel or boarding house. For the next couple of days they would again use a taxi to visit all the shops and businesses in the villages, (Beragh, Sixmilecross and Seskinore) and to the many little country shops scattered around the district. Their job was to collect money and take orders for more supplies. They also advised on any new product that became available.

In the mornings the stations, the goods yard and sheds would have been hubs of activity as workers and secondary school pupils hurried on their way and bread-servers arrived to fill their carts or vans with bread. Quite a number of the bread-men were still using horse drawn breadcarts in my early days.

Barney Kelly, Peter Bennett and Billy Harvey delivered Inglis bread. Their vans were horse drawn until about 1932. As sales increased, a fourth (motorised) van was supplied. Sean Bennet, son of Peter, drove it. In later years as the older men retired, their vans were taken over by Stanley McDonald, Michael O'Kane, Mick McCartan and Bertie McFarland.

While Inglis bread would seem to have been the most popular for a time, there was plenty of choice available. John Boyle delivered Winsor bread. McComb's bread was delivered by Jack Todd. Pat Heaney (and later his son Jack) sold Barney Hughes's bread.

Jimmie McSorley delivered Stevenson's bread for many years. After his passing Eugene Bogan took charge. He too died young and Declan Grimes took over for a while. Thomas Dillon sold bread baked in The Model Bakery. Barney Harte's van carried the Co-Op bread. Willie McLaren was the last man to drive a horse drawn bread-cart. He sold Brewster's bread. He later got a small electric or battery powered van. Felix McCann took over when Willie died. Frankie Kelly too, had a van on the road. He sold Eton's bread. In later years, the Ormo Bakery delivered bread in the district. About half of these vans collected the bread at the railway station. Others filled up at the bakeries or at depots.

As very few people owned cars in those days, newly wed couples who could afford a honeymoon, were escorted to the railway station by their guests. Indeed it was a good few years after the war before the vast majority could enjoy this luxury.

# Smuggling

Younger people today might wonder why it was necessary to board the train to go to Bundoran. It should be understood that very few people owned cars back then. Furthermore anyone who was lucky enough to own a car was required to have a pass stamped at the border checkpoint each time they crossed over. They were also expected to declare any purchases they had made. But while the restrictions at that time made life difficult for many it provided young able-bodied men who lived near to the border with a challenge. Good money could be earned if you had the time and energy to spare. It was really surprising how many items that were easily obtained in the South were rationed in the North, while other articles, readily available in the North, were difficult to procure south of the border.

Since all road users were obliged to stop at the customs check posts smuggling by road was not recommended. But there were other options. Those who were born in close proximity to the border were not very old when they knew quite a number of paths through the fields which led across the imaginary border line that separated North from South. Men of my age, and some who are much younger, can relate great stories of the goods they carried and the animals they drove along these paths in the dark of night. Driving cattle along these paths was no mean feat especially on nights when there was no moonlight, and, I am told by men who had the experience, that it was much more difficult to drive a litter of pigs. The course of a river or a stream is often used as the borderline between North and South. While pigs may wallow in mud they seem to detest water and only those who knew the tricks of the trade were able to persuade them to wade in and cross over the border streams.

Carrying turkeys across the border in the weeks before Christmas was a task for a strong, able young man. I doubt if the method used in olden days would get the blessing of the R.S.P.C.A. today. Each man or lad was supposed to carry four birds. The legs of two turkeys were tied together and they were hung over a man's right shoulder, one bird hanging to the front and the other hanging down his back. Two more turkeys were placed in similar fashion on the left shoulder and then it was time to go. While the method was most certainly painful for the turkeys it was by no means pleasant for the carrier either, as the birds sharp claws often scratched his neck or ears.

Eggs were smuggled in large numbers. A box or case held thirty dozen and while some were content to make the journey with one box it was not unknown for a man to carry two boxes, one slung on his back and one to his chest. But for the most part cases of eggs were wheeled on bicycles. I am told that at one stage in the wartime it was possible to earn £1 by moving a case of eggs from the South to the North. A pound was considered as a lot of money back in those days. In later years the young men got more adventurous and purchased an old van. While it was possible to move more goods in this manner it meant one had to acquire knowledge of the movements of the police and of the customs officials. Even with this knowledge it was not possible to evade capture on the odd occasion and one had to pay the price.

Smuggling in a small way was not considered a crime in those far off days and a small number of smuggled calves would have found a new home on most farms in the North in the years before identity tags were introduced. In later years, and for animal health reasons, the vast majority of farmers abided strictly by the rules.

# Ghosts at Midnight

Long ago in the days and nights before we had cars or electric light, ghosts and stories about ghosts played a big part in keeping young people (and indeed quite a number of older folk) indoors on the dark winter nights. I never did see or encounter a ghost, but to be truthful, as a young lad I was often scared stiff. A light in an unfamiliar place, a shadow that moved, or a strange noise could send shivers up one's spine. If chains were heard rattling it was a sure sign that the devil was out to get you. In bygone days most old disused houses or sheds were said to be haunted. One explanation as to why older people told these stories was to deter courting couples from meeting there, as was the custom before cars became plentiful.

Even to this day we sometimes hear of houses where unexplained happenings are still said to occur and once again I can truthfully confirm that I have no desire to investigate the matter. I know of two or three old houses in the district which were said to be haunted. When I was still quite young I often had to pass close to the gable of one of them. In the days long before I was born, this house was the home of a landlord who was, to put it mildly, most unkind to his tenants. Then, during the last decade of the nineteenth century and the first decade of the twentieth, Land Acts were passed and most tenants got the opportunity to buy or become the owner of the farm they had previously rented. Now, it was widely known that in the old landlord's house, which was not far from our home, there was a room that no-one entered. In fact, the door was always locked. In that room it was rumoured there was a tightly corked bottle which contained an evil spirit. This spirit was supposed to have been ordered into the bottle in an exorcism ceremony many years before. When the landlord vacated the house it lay empty for a period of time. During this interval a group of young lads dared each other to break into the house and find the bottle. Four or five of the group took up the challenge and succeeded in finding a tightly corked bottle. After many deliberations as to how to dispose of the bottle and its contents it was decided to put it on top of a pillar and use it as a 'cockshot'. This they did, but it was quite some time before a stone struck the bottle. The old man who told the story was one of the group. He explained how the bottle had burst with a mighty loud bang and a big puff of black smoke went up into the air and travelled away west. Believe it or not, after that escapade the house and farm were sold. I knew the new owners and they never did occupy the room. In later years the farm was resold and a new dwelling was built. The old house still stands but is now unoccupied.

Another story that I have heard repeated many times. It concerns a priest and his jarvey as they returned home on a winter's evening. They were coming down the road through the "Glushey" into Sixmilecross. The Glushey or "Glisha" is a stretch of soft marshy ground between the road and the old railway near to the village. Both claim that they were coming along and the pony was at a nice steady trot when suddenly the whole caboodle; priest, jarvey, pony and trap, were all lifted off the ground, swirled around a couple of times and dropped down in the field. Luckily they landed right end up but the jarvey was shivering like a leaf. When he got his breath back he looked at the priest and in a stammering voice he said, "Do you know Father, I think the aul' devil isn't too far away". "Maybe not" said the priest, "but sure, God is not far away either". Pointing to the gate he said, "Open that and drive on". I would be telling a lie if I said I knew the old priest well. I think I saw him once but he died a couple of years after I started school.

During the years of the war and the blackout I did manage to get a couple of nasty frights. The date is not important but at that time we had pictures in the Parochial Hall every Sunday and Thursday night. I seldom or never missed a show. Most nights I would walk or run into the village. On rare occasions I would have a bicycle. I mentioned somewhere that two roads led out from the village and joined again about half a mile outside. For some reason which I can't explain I used one road if I was walking and the other one if I had the bike. There was one farmhouse along the road which I walked and in it lived two old men. One was the owner of the farm and the other had been a helper but was now old and crippled. His name was Hughie Moore. Hughie quite often called into the village for a drink and on my way home I would often find him struggling along or maybe leaning on the Railway Bridge waiting for a helping hand. He would catch my arm and we would shuffle along the few hundred yards to his home. I didn't mind, as any company was welcome when one was walking alone in the dark. The road we walked was two or three hundred yards from the river but the ground was flat. This meant that at a time when we had a big flood, water backed up and the drains at the roadside would fill up.

On one particular Thursday when we'd had a lot of rain, I went to the pictures on my bicycle and travelled on the wider road. Early next morning we learned that Hughie Moore was dead. The poor man had fallen into the water filled drains by the roadside and was drowned. I felt awful although I knew that Hughie had often gone to and come from the village without my assistance but the incident was still on my mind especially on the next Thursday night. I didn't like the idea of walking past the spot where the poor old man had died so I took the bike and travelled the other road.

On my way home after the pictures, my mind was still very much on old Hughie's tragedy. Then, just exactly at the spot where the two roads join, I was peddling along when I got a fierce tug on my left side and I fell onto the grass verge with my head close to the hedge. For the next few seconds as I lay there I did believe in ghosts, worse still I was sure one had come to get me. When I struggled to get up I could not, I seemed to be tied to the bike. It took me quite a long time to discover what had happened. In bygone days we wore long overcoats. Mine had a belt, which I had not buckled. One end had fallen down and, as I peddled along, it got caught between the chain and the gear wheel and dragged me off. Mind you, I am still not thoroughly convinced that Hughie did not have a hand in it.

My second encounter with a ghost was much less dramatic. It happened near the end of our own lane. It was a moonlit night but not very clear. I was walking, probably to the village, when I saw a light in the undergrowth of the hedge. I walked past it giving it a good wide berth. I did not go far until I stopped. I knew I had to pass it again on my way home so I might as well deal with it there and then. Slowly I moved back. It was still there, a small glimmer of light, little better than a spark. It didn't move and I moved very slowly. It wasn't a flame but it was shining through the grass and the undergrowth. I thought it might be wise to get some help but I knew that if the light disappeared before I got back, I would surely be laughed at. I thought of throwing a stone at it but if it disappeared I would never know what it was.

I ventured to put my hand down and move some of the grass and still there was no movement of the light. As I got closer I got a bit more courage and finally I put my hand over to the spot where the light was shining. It was then I discovered what a fool I had been. It was a bicycle lamp. My sister had taken it of her bicycle one day when she was going shopping and when she returned she could not find the spot where it was hidden. The rain or dampness must have acted as a switch and caused the light to glow. Anyhow, my second ghost was another fake.

Another visitor that could spoil your night's sleep was the banshee. Sometimes a pale-faced céilíer would enter a house claiming he had heard the banshee. Then not only would there be a lengthy discussion about who in the district was the most likely to be on their way to their eternal reward but the faint-hearted in the house would make sure they would have someone to accompany them on their way home. No doubt there were several false alarms. Strangely enough, to this present day, I know a few people who really and truly believe that they have heard the banshee and they would be deeply offended if someone were to hint that it was their imagination.

Jamey Fa was the oldest man I have ever known. His proper name may have been James Farr but no one I knew called him by that name. He lived in the townland of Roscavey close to where my grandparents had a small country shop. He had a great long white beard that covered his face and a big portion of his tattered waistcoat. He owned a small bit of land, seven or eight acres, and lived alone in a tiny house which consisted of one room and a kitchen. The outhouses had long since lost their roofs. His entire stock, a donkey, a cow and her calf, were given shelter in the room of his dwelling in the wintertime. His few hens roosted on the backs of chairs or on the rail at the bottom of his bed that was near to the fire in the kitchen.

At one stage a neighbour alerted the local doctor and told him of the conditions in which the old man lived. The doctor duly called and suggested to the old man that he would be much better off in a home but Jamey had no intention of leaving the home in which he was born. Later in the day, my uncle called and the old man's words were, "But, but, I had a scut in here a while ago". Year's later Jamey did get ill and was confined to bed in his own home. Neighbours took turns to stay with him at night time. Finally, on a winter evening just as darkness was falling, my uncle and another neighbour, James McCollum, (both men are now dead) were in the house with the sick man when they heard a faint whining sound down in the glen which was close at hand. Slowly the whining got louder as it approached the house. It was at its peak as it passed the window and stopped for a moment or two at the door before moving on and fading into the night.

My uncle told me that both he and his companion sat dumb-founded while the whining lasted and that it was moments later his comrade broke the silence and said, "It will not be long now". He then got up from his chair and went over to the bed where he found the old man had passed away. Both men left immediately and contacted the clergy, the undertakers and the neighbours, who gathered and waked the deceased as was (and still is) customary in this locality. Both men would testify that they had heard the banshee.

The Willo-the-wisp was another hazard of the night. It was claimed that he carried a light and led people astray, often causing them to walk around in a field for hours before they could find their way home. "I must have stepped on a stray sod," was another phrase that was used by many who arrived home late and claimed they had walked miles and could not find the gate or opening, or as many would have said, the 'gap' out of the field. Satellite navigation was not available back then.

Dare I chance boring some readers by mentioning fairies? Well I did know two men who still believed in fairies. Not only did I know them but I céilíed in their old home. They were brothers, Paddy and Peter Bann. Campbell was their proper surname but no one would know who you were talking about if you mentioned that name. Every one of the neighbours knew that they believed in fairies but in every other way they were regarded as the smartest men in the townland, and it was a big townland. Their advice was sought when cattle were to be bought or sold, or when animals were sick and needed to be 'dosed' (given medicine).

Paddy was stiff and lame when I knew him but he could still help to milk the cows and do the housework. He could bake a scone of bread or make the dinner as well as any housewife, and better than some. Peter worked with the horses and attended to all other jobs on the farm. In the middle of a field on their farm and near to their house a lone hawthorn bush grew. Both men would have claimed to have seen the fairies dancing around that tree and to have heard the music. Woe-be-tide the person who would dare take a twig of that tree. On one occasion when both men were at a fair some of their young cattle strayed onto the roadway. A helpful passer-by put them back to their field. To repair the fence he unwittingly cut a branch of the lone tree. When the brothers returned from the fair they claimed to have found the cows jumping about and in danger of breaking the stalls in the byre, and the horse was wrecking the stable. Nothing the men could do would pacify the beasts until they heard about the branch being cut from the lone tree. In great haste they collected the branch and took it back to the tree and tied it back in place. Within minutes the animals calmed down and all was peaceful once more.

Now, half a mile down the road and on the other side, fairies of a different temperament were said to reside in a glen. This glen was on land owned by the late Bernard Hepburn, better known as Wee Barney. I remember him as a wee small man with a head of longish curly hair and a moustache. I don't think he lived to be very old but I never saw him do any work. As he walked along he always hummed a wee tune. The story was that the fairies had switched babies when Barney was an infant and that neighbours had searched for days to find the real child. Be that as it may, the fairies in that glen were said to be feared while the group that danced at the lone tree were friendly. Could it be that the townland of Roscavey was the last staging post for the fairies in Ireland? Paddy's and Peter's mother lived to be a very old woman. She told how, early each morning, a very small woman would call at her door.

She carried a tiny little can and she would ask for some milk.

On her last call she told the old lady that she might not be seeing her anymore. She explained, "Tonight we go to battle. If we win, I will be back. But if we lose, your well will be red with blood tomorrow morning". The following morning the water in the well was red.

# The Road Man

Today, the 29th March 2006, I listened to a phone-in debate on Radio Ulster about the condition of our roads. Callers rang in from all over the six counties complaining about the desperate state of the roads in their respective localities. There was little doubt that their complaints were genuine judging from the condition of roads in our own area. Such discussions tend to provoke memories of how road works were carried out over sixty years ago. For most part the County Council contracted out the task of keeping rural or country roads in repair to local men. These men were usually small farmers. My father was one such person. Unfortunately I cannot lay hand on any written documents clarifying the contracts but I am fairly well acquainted with what they contained.

The contractor was obliged to provide x number of cubic yards of stone, broken to a specified size, in depots on the roadside. They also had to be available at the depots on a pre-arranged date and time to assist the surveyor in examining and measuring the stones. Then, usually in the autumn, when the County Council made the steamroller available, the contractor was required to have sufficient manpower at hand so as to have the work finished in an allotted time. Extra time was at the contractor's expense.

The steamroller arrived towing a fireman's caravan, a bogie[8] for coal and a watering cart. The fireman started early in the morning, often before six o'clock. His tasks were to clean, oil and grease the steamroller, and light the fire so as to have full steam up when it was time to start. The driver then took over. At least three horses were required when the work started. One was to haul the water cart, which was a tank fixed to the frame of a cart. It also had a pump attached. It was taken to the nearest stream and filled with water. Two horses and carts fetched stones from the depots to the spot where they were required. Here two men using shovels levelled the stones evenly on the road. A third man dug clay from the grass verge and threw it over the stones. If clay was not available at the spot it had to be found and carted there. The man with the watering cart then sprayed water on the clay until it was thin mud and did not stick to the roller. The steamroller then rolled the patch while the workers went ahead to a different spot. When the roller had crushed the stones into the road, men with brushes were left to brush and clean the spot, and repair the grass verge to the best of their ability. More than seventy five percent of the stones were required to be rolled in; the remainder was reserved to fix potholes as they occurred during the year.

## *Driving*

*Sure it's no longer safe to be out on the roads,*
*With the speed of the cars and big lorries with loads.*
*When you drive at sixty they still want to get past*
*If you do not pull over the horn gets a blast.*

The double white line might as well not be there,
They just swerve out and pass and they don't seem to care.
Some were seen driving between rows of cones
With one hand on the wheel and their ears to their phones.

Sometimes in the evening or perhaps late at night
If you were out walking you could well get a fright
When some lad starts drifting and heats up his tyre
It will smell as if rubber has burned in the fire.

He'll turn with the hand brake where there is no need
And before he's right straightened he takes off at speed
He makes the tail wriggle and the big engine roar
As he gives it more juice with his foot to the floor.

Cars are so handy for getting around
But there's no parking space when we go to town
I've gave it some thought, it really is funny
City folk don't want us, they just want our money

Leabharlanna Poibli Chathair Bhaile Átha Cliath
Dublin City Public Libraries

The woman of the house too had a busy day. At least one substantial meal was required to be cooked and conveyed to where the men were at work, sometimes five or more miles from home. Cups were sent in the cart in the morning but the hot meal was packed in two boxes and tied on the carrier of two bicycles. My teenage sisters then pushed the bikes to where the men were working. I, being slightly younger, only qualified once for this task. We all were anxious to be allowed to go as we were allowed to ride the bikes on the homeward journey.

The day the steamroller came was far from being the only hard days work required to keep the road in repair for twelve months. First of all, stones had to be provided. This was often done by gathering them off the cornfields soon after the corn was sown and the green shoots were to be seen - in farmer's language, when the corn 'brearded'. These stones were carted to the depots on the roadside and many days were spent breaking them with stone hammers. Each stone was supposed to be small enough to go through a two-inch ring. If sufficient stones were not acquired this way some more had to be raised in a stone quarry. This was done with picks and sledgehammers and was very heavy work.

'Vennels', or water channels, and outlets were required to be kept open so as to prevent water lying on the roadway. Weeds, grass and briars were cut with scythes or shearing hooks and the grass verges trimmed back at least once a year. The road was expected to be swept and kept clean at all times. If no penalty was imposed for faulty work, or neglect, the contractor could expect to receive about twenty five or maybe thirty pounds for keeping three or four miles of roadway in repair for twelve months.

Trunk roads were the only roads that had a tarred surface in the first half of the last century and the method of tarring was laborious, dangerous and slow. The Council employees usually did this work. They used a horse drawn tar pot or tar boiler fitted with a man-operated winch and a rotary type pump. The tar was brought to the site in forty-gallon drums. Two men turning the handle of the winch lifted these on to the tar pot. A hole was chopped in one end with an axe to allow the tar to flow into the boiler and a coal fire underneath brought the tar to boiling point. Then one man stood close to the boiler and operated the pump while another held a long hose and sprayed the tar on to the road. Two or three men using shovels spread fine stones or screenings over the tar and the roller pressed them in. The worker who held the hose and sprayed the tar wore hob nailed boots and had meal bags tied around his legs to prevent the boiling tar from burning him.

Today's health and safety regulations would no doubt prohibit work being carried out in this manner but we never heard of an accident or any big claims. It was a cruel job on a hot summer's day when the temperature rose to thirty degrees.

A by-product or spin off from the tarring of the roads was the empty drums that had held the tar. At that time these were known as 'coalis drums'. As a matter of fact, I understand that the contents of the drums were known as coalis, not tar. Anyhow the drums seemed to be non-returnable. They were in big demand by farmers and householders. When the tops and bottoms were removed from the drums they were cut down the side at the seam and flattened out. They were then used as cladding for turf or hay sheds. They can be seen in some places to the present day.

# The Hired Hand

From time to time we often find it necessary to hire a car to do a journey, or some implement to do a certain job about the house or garden. In bygone days, up until 1940, hiring usually had a different meaning. Until then hiring usually meant that servants were employed to help in the home or on the farm or shop for a period of time for an agreed sum of money. Back in those days the agreements were usually made in the hiring fairs which were held in most towns and villages in the months of May and November each year. As soon as an agreement was made it was usual for the employer to give the employee one shilling which made the contract binding. Servants who, without a very good reason, left their job before the agreed time risked losing all their pay.

On the 19th November 1928 a young girl was hired to work in a shop in Sixmilecross. As was the saying at that time, she was to 'live in' and be treated as one of the family. A list was kept of each and every expense that she incurred. When she was leaving the job to get married exactly ten years later and a settlement of her contract was being made, figures show that she was due to receive £4-17s-4d. Out of the goodness of their hearts they gave her £5- 0s-0d.

Many young girls who were hired to work in farmhouses earned only half the pay that a shop girl received and they would have had heavier and dirtier work to contend with. The average six monthly pay for female workers in the nineteen thirties was five or six pounds if they ate and slept on the premises. Male hired workers received slightly more, usually eight to ten pounds. A man capable of working with horses might get a couple of pounds more. Apart from being poorly paid many were poorly treated. In several houses, workers were not allowed to sit at the same table as the family and were expected to be content with less palatable food.

An old neighbour of mine, the late Willie Anderson, told of an experience a time long ago when he was leaving the hiring fair with his little bundle of clothes on his shoulder. A farmer with a horse and cart offered him a lift. The farmer enquired of Willie where he was going. Willie told him the name of the man who had hired him and the directions he was given. There was silence for a moment and then the farmer asked. "Can you eat hay?" Willie didn't understand what he meant at the time but he found out before he was long at the job.

Another man I knew worked for a Mr. Jordan. Both are long since dead and gone. At this farmhouse the meals were few and far between but the young worker was quick to find a good supplement. As he helped to milk the cows he got a long straw and put one end into his mouth and the other end into the bucket. Then as he milked he was able to suck the milk up through the straw. The farmer often complained about how poor a milker the cow was and often threatened to sell her.

Many Donegal workers found employment in this district. Not far from our home a Donegal girl was hired to work on a larger than average sized farm. She had been there for some time when two local lads were employed to do some building. One morning they were working on a scaffold which was only about four or five foot high. In fact it was only three or four long wooden planks placed on top of two forty gallon beer barrels. The girl was passing by with two buckets of feed for the hens. One of the lads turned round as she came by and said, "Hi Maggie, would you be a good girl and hand me up the bucket of mortar that's sitting there". Now, he probably did not expect her to do it, rather he wanted to hear what she would say, but without hesitation Maggie left down one bucket of hen's food, lifted the bucket of mortar, and putting her right knee to the side of the bucket she hoisted it up. The lad on the scaffold was ill-prepared for such a quick response, and he had no choice but to grab the handle of the bucket. He was completely off balance when Maggie let go of the handle and down he came, head first, at her feet. Luckily there was nothing hurt but his pride and as soon as he got to his feet Maggie went on to feed the hens. They became friendly later, but it was on Maggie's terms.

On some of the bigger farms where two or more hired workers were employed, accommodation was provided for them in an old farmhouse. The hearth fire in this house was also used during the day to boil potatoes and other animal foods. Many of the workers preferred this arrangement, especially on the long winter nights. I understand that there were restrictions on whom the workers could allow into the building and also a time set for "lights out".

Farmers, and indeed many other employers, preferred the hired hands to come from a distance. The reason for this was that it made it difficult, if not impossible, for them to go home at the weekends. When they stayed over they were expected to give a hand on Sundays.

I doubt if there are many alive today that worked as a hired hand in their youth. Soon after the start of the Second World War it became compulsory to pay workers and stamp their card each week. Few local farmers were in a position to meet this demand but workers were slightly better off even though their weekly pay was still a pittance.

## Forty days and forty nights.

*In the year of Our Lord two thousand and seven,*
*God wasn't impressed when he looked down from Heaven.*
*He saw the whole world was in a bad state,*
*Mankind was behaving quite badly of late.*
*Every where that he looked there was some kind of bother,*
*Men were at war and killing each other.*
*Woman folk, too, must bear part of the blame,*
*The way some behave, it is really a shame.*

*George Bush wants the oil in Iran and Iraq,*
*He was asked, but refused to call the troops back,*
*There's war in Afghanistan and in Egypt too,*
*Countries at peace are relatively few.*
*Not long ago, we had violence and hate,*
*Thank God for the peace and quiet of late.*
*But young ones still binge drink and carry a knife,*
*If you got in their way they might take your life.*

*So when God looked down and saw all the pain,*
*He sighed and lamented, I may send down more rain.*
*So, He said unto Noah, "Go, build me an ark,*
*The behaviour down there is no longer a lark.*
*Of all beasts of the earth, take two of each kind,*
*Of the people, four couples, the best you can find.*

The birds of the air, of each species take two,
As all fish can swim, they will find oceans new".

"Collect insects and crawlies; gather all that you can,
And listen now carefully, this is my plan,
In exactly one year I will call back again,
If everything's ready, I'll send down the rain.
For forty days steady, the rain will pour down,
Until it has covered every inch of the ground.
Not even a hilltop will there be in sight,
Grey clouds in the sky will block out the light".

God called back in twelve months, but no ark could he see,
He said, "My friend Noah, just how can this be?"
"Lord forgive me," said Noah "but I did my best,
Never once in the past year did I stop for a rest.
I have gave of my time and procured all the tools,
But, Good Lord of Heaven, just look at these rules.
Hundreds of documents, all filled without fail,
But I must wait for permission before I drive a nail".

"Red tape in this auld world has really gone mad,
It's no longer a joke, it surely is sad.
Building control just laughed at my plan,
Saying, who needs an ark in the midst of dry land?
Environmentalists defied me to cut any trees,
Accused me of endangering the birds and the bees,
Neighbours claim that a vessel as big as the ark,
Would block out the light and leave them in the dark".

"Trade unions claim my sons can't help with the scheme,
And we're told, the disabled, must be part of the team.
Fire Authorities demand that the ark has a sprinkler,
And Traffic Control avows we must have a tinkler.
Animal Health is resolved that we carry two vets,

*One for large animals and one for the pets.*
*But, worst of all, you could hardly surmise,*
*My assets were frozen by the Customs and Excise".*

*"I'm sorry," said Noah, "but I did my best,*
*But I doubt t'would take years to manage the rest".*
*God thanked him kindly, saying he understood,*
*But the future for earthlings did not look very good.*
*"Then will you destroy it?" Noah ventured to ask,*
*"For I am quite willing to finish the task".*
*"Thank you kindly" God answered, "We'll leave it on the shelf,*
*The way man is behaving he will do it himself".*

# Have a 'Brash'

Even for those of us who are old enough to remember, it is still difficult to understand how so much change can have taken place in a lifetime. Prior to World War II there would seem to have been little change in the methods of working or in lifestyles in the previous century. In the 1930s, work was still very routine and labour intensive. Mechanisation was in its infancy and electricity had reached only the towns. Manual labour was the order of the day. Milking the cows was done by hand and ten cows would have been considered a large herd; five would probably have been the average. The horse and cart took the milk to the creamery where it was measured (gallons and pints) and separated. The cream was kept for churning and the separated part of the milk was poured back into the milk can and taken home to be fed to calves or pigs. On certain days of the week buttermilk was available and each farmer was offered his share. It too, was fed to calves and only milk churned at home was used for making bread or for drinking. It was sometimes used to make the oat meal porridge and was considered a treat.

A quantity of Sunday's milk was kept for churning. The dash churn was the most common in this district. Tuesday was usually churning day and it took about one hour. It was a job for two people. One churned for about five or six minutes and then rested while the other took over. Learning to churn properly took quite some time. At the changeover, the beginner had to learn to grasp the churn staff with both hands before the other person let go and to keep on churning at the same steady rhythm. The staff had to be lifted to the very top of the milk and then plunged to the bottom without splashing the milk. A five-minute turn at the churn was known as a 'brash'. If a neighbour called in while the churning was in progress it was considered lucky to allow him or her to give the churn a brash. When the butter formed it was lifted off and washed in cold spring water. It was then put into a wooden butter dish that had been thoroughly washed and rubbed with salt. It was patted with wooden butter spades until all the milk was removed. Salt was added and, lastly, portions weighing about one pound were placed on a decorative print and patted in to fancy shapes.

In the late 1930s, milk suppliers were obliged to apply for a Grade C licence. To obtain this licence, cow-byres were required to have a concrete floor, concrete partitions and walls plastered to a height of five foot. It was compulsory to have a dairy specifically for milk and the required milking utensils. At least two stainless steel buckets and a milk strainer were required. Ever since, the change to more modern methods has been unceasing.

Two-unit milking machines and in-churn milk coolers were introduced in this district in the late 1940s and the early 1950s. Then as electricity became more widely available, ice bank coolers were quick to follow. The next change was the introduction of stainless steel pipelines, which carried the milk straight from the cow to the milk churn in the dairy. Shortly afterwards milking parlours and bulk tanks were being installed on the bigger farms and soon these became common place. Rotary milking parlours have made their debut ten or more years ago but these are not afford-able on the average farm. I understand that three or four farms in the north of Ireland have invested in 'robot' milking parlours. In these the cow has free access at all times, she is milked automati-cally and her milk is recorded.

Our local creamery in Beragh closed in 1942 when the Nestlé factory opened in Omagh. The creamery had had a life span of about sixty years. Nestlé closed in the year 2000 with much the same life span. Since then milk is collected in huge tankers and goes we know not where.


## A Plea

*Nothing in, nothing out, that's an order*
*Not a beast to be moved on the land.*
*But Bríd, would you hold for a moment*
*This whole thing has got out of hand.*
*For you know the aul' barns are empty*
*And the walls of the silos are bare.*
*Sure even the aul' cows in the byre*
*Know that there's new grass out there*

*Have you not seen the daffodils blooming*
*As they gently sway in the breeze?*
*Have you failed to hear the dawn chorus,*
*As the little birds nest in the trees?*
*Have the lengthening days gone unnoticed*
*As the sun climbs high in the sky?*
*Even the swallows are returning*
*And the as trout as it jumps for the fly.*

*Bríd, you can't stop the pale moon from rising*
*Nor the flow or the ebb of the tide,*
*So why keep the poor cows from grazing?*
*Must they stand on hard concrete instead?*
*Beware, you can't hide from nature.*
*In time it will find its own way.*
*Disaster could strike you or miss you*
*Neither you nor I have a say.*

*We've befouled this world that we live in,*
*We seem driven by corruption and greed.*
*We risk our own health for the sake of great wealth*
*And ignore our poor neighbours in need.*
*Some folk get their moment of glory,*
*But somehow it soon fades away.*
*For man himself and all of his wealth*
*Must one day return to the clay.*

# Clocking Hens

Visiting old farmyards which were undisturbed since the 1930s, one is apt to find old cracked metal pots or similar utensils built into the stone walls of sheds or barns. More recently, one is likely to find a hammer or some small hand tools thrown into them, but their original purpose was as nesting places for hens to lay their eggs. In those bygone days, a dozen or two hens and a rooster around the barn door was a common sight, and these nesting places were usually close at hand. They would have been bedded with a little hay and a delph⁹ egg was placed in each one. This encouraged the hens to use the nests.

Occasionally a hen would stray off and lay her egg in a nest well hidden in a thick hedge or concealed in weeds behind a wall. If left undetected, the broody hen would one day appear with her brood of chicks. Usually, if the flock numbers needed to be increased, a 'setting' of eggs, thirteen in number, was got from a neighbouring farm. They were placed under a broody hen in a quiet corner, sometimes in an outhouse, but it was not uncommon to find one or more in a spare room of the dwelling house or indeed under a table in a pantry or scullery. Each day the hen would be lifted off and taken outside to be fed but as soon as she had eaten she would quickly return to her nest. After about twelve days, with the aid of a lighted candle, it was possible to find out which eggs were infertile and these were removed from the nest. Chicks took about 21 days to hatch. More often than not, an egg or two would be broken or a weak chick would fail to break through the shell. Consequently ten live chicks were considered a good hatch.

By the way, back in those days, broody hens were known as

'clockers'. So, while most clockers were great mothers to their chicks and would fight to protect them, they would also lead them into some filthy spots. Here they were prone to catch disease, the most common one being the 'roup'. In the dictionary roup is described as a 'kind of catarrhal inflammation of the eyes and the nasal passages'. It caused the chicks to stand gasping. Old people had two cures for the roup. One cure was to put two handfuls of dry lime into a shoebox, then the sick bird was placed inside and the lid put on tightly. The box then was given a good shake and the bird was allowed to stay inside for a moment or two. The second cure was even more severe. It was called 'feathering' the bird. To perform this operation one trimmed both sides of a feather leaving a small tuft on the top. Then holding the bird's head in one hand, the feather was pushed down its throat and turned round twice before being removed. Strange as it may seem, quite a few birds survived this operation. Still, mortality was high, and considering that of all chicks reared, about fifty per cent were cockerels,

it took quite a few 'settings' to keep up or increase the numbers. The demand for eggs and poultry grew rapidly when the war started in 1939. Incubators that had the capacity to hatch one hundred eggs were popular; still half of each hatch were cockerels and had to be disposed off as soon as they could be identified.

Soon it was discovered that buying day old sexed chicks from the hatchery was the better option. In many cases these chicks spent at least a week in the kitchen or a spare room of the farmhouse, as they needed heat and a great deal of attention day and night. After a week they were moved out to a wooden house in the green fields. For some time chicks were supplied true to each breed, such as White Leghorns, Brown Leghorns, Rhode Island

Reds, Bared Rock, Ancona, Sussex, or Whyn Dots. Accredited farms were set up, each for a particular breed. They were all registered with the Ministry of Agriculture.

Poultry clubs were formed, meetings were held, excursions and outings were arranged. Portable hen arks and wooden hen houses grew in numbers and could be seen in most fields as the hens scattered free range from dawn to dusk. Eggs were no longer carried to the shops in baskets but packed, thirty dozen in a box or 'case' and collected in lorries. On most farms the housewife was in charge of the hens and after many years of scraping and saving, they had a few shillings to spare. Soon the number of cases of eggs produced each week was part of every conversation.

As the shillings accumulated and became pounds, the odd second-hand car soon began to appear on the country roads. The engine in quite a few of the cars of that time could be difficult to restart if allowed to stop before it became properly warmed up. A family who lived some miles outside Sixmilecross purchased one such vehicle. Soon after it arrived at its new home, the young driver stopped at the top of a hill to chat to a pal. Now this hill, known locally as Caldragh[10], is very steep and about half a mile long. When the pals had finished their chat and the driver decided to move on. The car refused to start. Several attempts were made but without success. Now the obvious thing to do was to let it run down the hill and surely it would start on the way. But that was not to be. When it reached the bottom of the hill the engine had failed to pick up and the car had to be towed away. A jealous neighbour who witnessed the procedure was heard to comment, "Sure the car is only a dud. My goodness, you could start an egg-box if you pushed it down Caldragh".

The boom in the poultry industry created many spin-off jobs. Of these, providing portable wooden henhouses was top of the list. During the war a permit was required to purchase timber. This meant that home-grown timber was in great demand. Tragically many trees and shelterbelts fell to the woodsman's axe. But the timber got no time to dry out or season. So streamlined was the set-up that a wood log could be sawn into suitable bits of timber and a new henhouse could be built and ready for sale in an eight hour working day. Unfortunately this type of house soon became draughty, as the newly sawn timber dried out and the seams opened. Often the door became ill fitting and it was not uncommon to hear of a fox raiding a hen house and killing a number of chickens.

Yet again, the system only lasted twelve or fifteen years until changes were in sight. It was always accepted that as the days grew shorter in the autumn, egg production would gradually drop. Then someone noticed that a few hens had roosted each night in a house where there was a light, and these continued to produce eggs well into the winter. Further research showed that, if a hen got sixteen hours light each day, she would continue to produce eggs for almost twelve months. So a lighted 'tilly' lamp was hung in the henhouse for a few hours each night. This led on to the deep-litter and cages. In a short space of time all empty sheds and barns on farms were bedded with dried peat moss or wood shavings. Roosts and nests were fitted and in a couple of years scarcely a chick could be seen in the fields. Soon larger and specially designed houses were being erected to hold greater numbers of hens, and poultry farming became a specialised job.

Already tests, trials, and crossbreeding were being carried out by different firms and hatcheries, probably in conjunction with the Ministry of Agriculture, as they endeavoured to outpace each other in a race to produce a super hen. Today the vast majority of hens are hybrid, identified only by letters or numbers. They have never seen the light of day. In fact it could be said that close to thirty generations of birds have never seen daylight. Their allotted space on earth is about one square foot. Their responsibility, to lay at least three hundred eggs. Their life span is little more than a year and their final destination, a pet food can.

A major portion, if not the entire poultry industry, is now controlled by three or four big firms and some henhouses have the capacity to hold one hundred thousand birds. These houses have no natural light. Broiler fowl, or those bred and reared for the table, have even a bleaker outlook. Their life span is a mere six weeks and in this short time they can reach weights of five, six or even seven pounds. They grow so fast that in some cases their legs are so weak that they cannot stand up.

Today we hear a lot of talk about obesity in people, especially the young. Could it be possible that the manner in which food is produced might in some way be a factor in this problem?

## The Clocking Hen

When my grandma was young, and a long time before,
The hens often perched on the little half door.
'Twas still much the same until my young day,
We'd be sent out to chase them and hunt them away.

But when war broke out and the food it got scant,
With the hens all around we were never in want.
With an egg on your plate at the start of the day,
It sure helped a lot to keep hunger at bay.

If we needed some meat, now sometimes there was naught,
We just plucked an auld rooster, and put him in the pot.
The feathers were gathered; they made pillows so soft
For the big iron bed up on the half loft.

And the bits that were left, now they would be few,
For the very last bone the auld doggie would chew.
Away in those days the auld folk could get cross,
If they thought for one moment we had put things to loss

When the food got real scarce, great was the demand.
Soon the hens were all scattered out over the land.
In wee wooden houses there were nests where they'd lay
From a hen you'd expect an egg every day.

But the days get much shorter, when it comes to the fall,
By the hooky, the hens would not lay then at all.
It seems the works in a hen will not function at night,
So we built deep-litter houses and gave them a light.
In no time at all they got back in gear,
And, by Jove, they kept laying for most of the year.

When the craft was perfected, big meal firms got greedy,
And stole the industry from the poor and the needy,
'Twill ne'er be the same, as we knew it back then,
When chickens were hatched 'neath an auld clocking hen.

# Fair Days and Dealers

It's a good number of years since I perused the pages of Old Moore's Almanac and the long columns of days and dates of cattle and horse fairs throughout Ireland. I doubt if the farmers and dealers of those bygone days had need to consult a calendar to reassure them of the exact days of fairs in their neighbouring towns or villages. Sixmilecross fair was held on the nineteenth day of each month. As it was the closest to home, it was where we usually sold our cattle. I was still young then and my duties were to help drive the animals to the fair and not allow them to mix with other cattle. This was not difficult to do as they were mostly tired after their three mile walk, but it could be quite annoying when a 'guinea-hunter' came along and prodded the best animal out from between it's comrades and demanded to know, "How much are you asking for the wee stirk?".

Fair Day at Ballygawley.

Sellers were often unsure of the value of their animals and if they under-valued their beast the guinea-hunter offered a much lower price or made a smart remark. He then hastened off to a dealer of his acquaintance and told him where he could get a good bargain, hoping to be rewarded if a deal materialised. For the benefit of those readers not familiar with dealers' language, a 'stirk' was a small calf and a 'guinea-hunter' was an impostor, who went around the district spotting bargains, getting involved in deals and hoping to receive a tip, or as some would say, a backhander.

*Making the deal*

I remember being at Sixmilecross fair one day when cattle were being herded on the footpath. One animal seemed to get inquisitive and ventured in through the front door of a private house. The owner of the animal instructed his son to go around to the back door and come through the house and put the calf out. Seconds later the young lad emerged, wide eyed, from the door next to the one the beast had entered. By then the lady of the house had heard the commotion and with the aid of a broom had removed the uninvited visitor, and had given the owner a bit of unwanted advice.

Shopkeepers, traders and pub owners welcomed fair days but private house owners detested them. The late Maggie Duffy stood in her doorway with a broom held with both her hands and woe-be-tide the man or beast that came within her range. On the day of the fair, two or three housewives in the village converted their parlours into tearooms and, with the help of willing friends and neighbours; they fed the multitude and earned a few shillings.

Omagh fair was held on the first Monday of each month, on a bit of rough ground at Gallows Hill. I was only there once but I remember the occasion well because of an episode that occurred on our way there. My father and my uncle had ten or twelve acres of grazing land taken in conacre[11] at Ranelly, right along the main Ballygawley to Omagh road.

*Dealers*

A dozen or so cattle were grazing there and, on an October morning back in 1943, four of us went there to drive six calves to Omagh fair. Two went in front of the animals and the two older men walked behind them. Traffic was not too heavy as we went in the Dublin road and turned up at Anderson's corner.

At that time, the County Cinema occupied the space where SuperValu Shopping Centre now stands. It had a long wide foyer where dozens of patrons queued up prior to being admitted to the pay box area. At the far end of the foyer were four or maybe six swinging glass doors, which led into the cinema proper. At this point on the street, traffic was quite heavy and something caused the calves to bolt, all six of them, straight down the cinema foyer. I was closest to the entrance but when I got there I was just in time to see the glass doors still swinging, but not a calf in sight. When the last of the drovers got the length of the entrance we all looked at each other but no one spoke for a moment. Each one of us was well aware of the damage the animals could do, or the mess they could make if they reached the seats and, anyway, our footwear was most unsuitable for treading on carpet. But we had not long to wait. Suddenly the glass doors burst open and out came the six cattle, tip-tapping up the foyer and out onto the street. We never found out how far they had gone or who or what turned them. Maybe they did not like the show. Anyhow we did get them to the fair hill without further incident. Trade was poor that day. The cattle were sold but did not reach their target price.

At that time there were very few lorries of any type in this district and definitely no cattle lorries. All cattle were made to walk to fairs; many had to travel long distances. Some farmers made arrangements with owners of land close to the fairground to allow them to bring the cattle to their land on the day prior to the fair. This way the cattle would be rested and have time to eat on the morning of the fair. Most fairs were held in towns or villages not far from a railway station and the majority of cattle-dealers availed of this service, though it was necessary to have cattle wagons ordered some time before the fair day.

There were exceptions however. It was not uncommon for cattle drovers to be given the task of driving animals from fairs forty or more miles away, and I have known quite a number of men who bought young horses in Ballybay fair, County Monaghan and walked home leading one, two or maybe three horses. I understand that it was against the law for one man to be in charge of any more than six horses on the road. He was allowed to have three in front walking abreast, followed by two, and then by one.

Sheep, too, were sometimes made to walk great distances but at a more leisurely pace. The title-holder for this feat in our district was the late Paddy McNamee of Remackin. Paddy was a sheep dealer. Towards the end of the summer and into early autumn, he would spend some time in the vicinity of Donegal town visiting the hill farms, or as he would have said himself, 'scouring the country' to buy sheep and lambs. When he had upwards of one hundred bought he would take them to the railway station, where he had a good relationship with the stationmaster who, for a very reasonable fee, would hook on an extra wagon for Paddy's sheep.

Unfortunately the railway authorities neglected to inform Paddy when they changed the stationmaster and Paddy's pleading could not sway the new man in charge. Even if he did have cash enough to pay the full fare, it was not in his nature to overspend if there was another option, and there was another way. It would take two or three days, maybe more, but there was no hurry. Paddy whistled, his faithful dog turned the sheep around and off they walked. Don't ask which road Paddy came home for he knew every byway and shortcut over a wide area. He knew exactly where he could get a night's grazing for his sheep, a bite for his dog and a place to lay his head. When he finally arrived home in Remackin, the sheep were allowed two or three weeks to rest and get their fleece cleaned up before starting out on the road again. This time the primary purpose of the expedition was to dispose of the flock. Paddy had a list of prospective buyers and a few lowland farmers would already have placed orders for a number of lambs.

Once more he knew exactly where to find a place of welcome and pasture for his flock as the shadows lengthened and another day was fast disappearing into the great abyss. Although his intended destination was the sheep sale at Markethill, Co. Armagh, Paddy never missed a chance to dispose of a few animals along the way if the price was right. It was easy to dispose of the last few lambs if prior sales were showing a good profit. It was seldom that Paddy's homeward journeys were uneventful. Somewhere along the way a new deal was usually waiting. It might only be a couple of goats or kids, or indeed, if it was close to home, a goose or two that were being sold cheap would not be left behind.

The mention of geese brings us on to another story. On only one occasion do I remember a goose and a gander at our house and the experiment must not have been a success, as I do not recall ever seeing goslings about the place. Geese are not very difficult to rear and require little or no housing but they are difficult to transport when full grown and ready for the Christmas market. When turkeys were tied in pairs it was possible to fit about twenty birds in the horse's cart. Not so with geese. Their legs were far too short to tie together and so they were sometimes driven to the market. Most farms in the neighbourhood had a flock of geese ready for the Christmas market and few had a bigger or better flock than the Nugent family of Remackin. The Nugents usually drove the geese to Sixmilecross market in mid-December. Here again there was a problem. The Nugent family lived about four miles from Sixmilecross and the Remackin River ran between their home and the market. Now, up until about 1960, there was no bridge. Only a narrow footbridge, or 'footstick' as it was called, spanned the twenty-foot wide river. This did not deter Paddy Nugent or his family.

Annually, in the days before Christmas, four members of the household drove the geese to the edge of the river close to the footbridge. Here two daughters, Peggy and Mary, took off their shoes and stockings and waded into the water to prevent the geese from going up or down stream. Their father and his other helper 'shushed' the geese to the opposite side and then walked across the footstick. The two girls then dried their legs, put on their footwear and continued to the market. At that time geese were sometimes driven unbelievable distances to market. An old neighbour of mine told me of seeing John Boyle of Beragh and a helper driving geese past Drumduff Chapel on their way to Beragh. They had started out near Gortin and bought geese at different houses as they walked along. Some of the geese would have walked almost fifteen miles. John was carrying one in his arms. It had given up on the way and there were still four or five miles to travel.

In mid-summer 1932, I remember my father buying a sow in Fintona fair. It was a hot summer's day and it took him hours driving her, and pushing his bicycle, on the ten-mile homeward journey. Two days later she gave birth to ten healthy piglets.

# Grants and Subsidies.

My earliest memories of Ministry Men or Agriculture Advisers go away back to the late 1930s. I had still a couple of years to stay at school but my eldest sister, who had just finished, went for a short time to help out in some emergency at the home of a Mr. Daly. He, I believe, was one of the first, and only, tillage inspectors in the Omagh area at that time.

Farming subsidies were still in their infancy back then. The only one I was aware of at that time amounted to the sum of one pound ten shillings per acre being offered to farmers for ploughing land that had not been tilled for at least seven years. This payment was rose to two pounds per acre in 1939 and again in 1949 it was raised to four pounds per acre. Food and animal feedstuffs were difficult to import during the war years and each farmer was compelled to plough fifty per cent of his arable land. In 1941 most foodstuffs had to be home-produced and potato growers were paid ten pounds subsidy per acre for well-tended crops. By 1945, the last year of the war, subsidies were raised to eighteen pounds per acre for potatoes, but it fell to eight pounds the following year. It was again raised to twelve pounds for the years 1948 and 1949, after which it was removed. From 1944 to 1949, three or four pounds per acre were available for crops of wheat or rye but the soil in this area was not suitable for either. Examining these facts we see that it took more than five years to recover after the war.

At this stage one might ask why did subsidies continue after food and all other commodities became plentiful once again after the war. The reason, we were told, was that foodstuffs would remain cheap and it would benefit the not-so-well-off. This was folly, as the well-to-do benefited in like manner. A more likely reason for the continuation of the system was the fact that, by the year 1947, the then Ministry of Agriculture had acquired offices in each of the six counties. A County Executive Officer, who had a full clerical staff and a number of field officers, controlled each of these offices. All offices had easy access to the head office in Belfast. Had the Ministry of Agriculture decided to dispense with the farm subsidies it would have meant paying off, or finding other employment for, hundreds of employees. For many years grants or subsidies were available for most aspects of farming. This included the demolition of old farm buildings and the erection of new modern ones. It also meant removing hedgerows and filling in many miles of the open drains. Hundreds of acres of mountain and bog lands were reclaimed and made into farmland. Furthermore the application of hundreds of thousands of tons of fertilizers, (sulphate of ammonia, potash, and phosphate) to farmland was encouraged and subsidised for well nigh fifty years.

Present day farming methods bear no resemblance to how work was done half a century ago. Silage-making was introduced in the late 1950s and early 1960s. In the early years generous grants were available for the erection of silos and a further payment was obtainable for every ton of silage made in the next two years. It's hard to believe, but true, that silage was being made for a number of years before even the Ministry inspectors were aware that the seepage from silage-making was deadly poisonous to fish stocks. From the earliest days of farming it was customary to tie the cows in stalls in a byre during the winter months. Now they were to be housed in big sheds within which they were allowed to roam and have free access to the silage. For a few years their lying area was bedded with straw but change came quickly. Slatted floors and slurry tanks were introduced and the cows had to adapt to lying in cubicles. Shortly afterwards all cows and pigs, were expected to spend most of their life on concrete and slatted floors.

The rearing of cattle for beef was also subsidised. So, too, was the production of milk. Subsidy on milk was not paid directly to the producer but to the firm that purchased the milk. This meant that milk used on the farm itself, either for feeding calves or milk used in the home, was not subsidized. Over the next number of years the age-old pattern of tillage farming was to gradually give way to grassland and silage. So thorough was the transformation that, since the turn of the century, scarcely an acre of tillage can be seen in our locality, or indeed in vast areas in the north and west of Ireland.

The truth is, subsidies and grants only distorted or disguised the true value of any product. Worse still, when subsidies were removed about ten years ago the monies the farmers received for many products did not cover the cost of production. In fact, money handed out in subsidies to farmers only passed through their hands and was quickly absorbed by supermarkets and other go-betweens. Subsidies also encourage fraud and deceit, and are likely to be of greater benefit to the unscrupulous. In many cases they are most beneficial to big-time smugglers.

## Hoodwinked

When I was a young lad and still going to school,
I first knew Frank Daly, now that man was no fool.
An Agriculture Adviser, the first of his kind,
A decenter fellow it would be hard to find.

Who sent him out, perhaps it was NATO?
His errand was about the humble potato.
Food was quite scarce then, 'twas the start of the war,
If you don't get your grub, you will not go far.

'Twas the Agricultural Department I believe sent him out,
And spuds were the things he was talking about.
He was doing his dead best to let all farmer's know,
We'd get £10 per acre, for the spuds we would grow.

Now ten pounds an acre was big money back then,
But when money comes handy it is easy to spend.
Soon we were encouraged to grow corn and wheat,
In fact to grow anything human beings would eat.

What I'm trying to tell you is hard to explain,
Although we worked harder we made little gain,
For on every item that we got grant aid,
Less was the money the producer was paid.

As the years rolled onwards the whole system got worse,
Till in fact at the finish the auld grants were a curse,
The producer was worse off than when they began,
Profit margins were used up by the middleman.

*Middleman is not the right word, I meant middlemen,*
*For in most of the cases there could be nine or ten.*
*When direct debit started things seemed to get worse,*
*For every last blighter had his hand in my purse.*

*The auld super-marts were giving farm produce away,*
*They weren't much out of pocket by the price that they paid.*
*Our goods were used as lost leaders to entice in the throng,*
*'Twas little they cared when they did us a wrong.*

*The Agriculture Department led all farmers astray,*
*Just coaxed them along with grants they did pay,*
*And when mad cow disease stopped the sale of the meat,*
*They then pulled the carpet from under our feet.*

*In so many ways their advice was not good,*
*And things did not turn out the way that they should,*
*From form-filling today there is no escape,*
*We're just bogged to the lugs in reams of red tape.*

# A Job for all Seasons

Those of us who were born in the second half of the 1930s have had the privilege of living through two vastly different lifestyles. In the first few years of our lives, although we were blissfully unaware, we lived through what is still referred to as the hungry thirties. These were years when lifestyles had changed little for a century and when money was scarce, almost non-existent. Undoubtedly our parents had difficult times but, as we lived on a small farm, we always had enough to eat and, as we were still young, we were not accustomed to luxuries. Our home was no different from our neighbours or other homes where there were children. No pair of shoes was disposed off until they could no longer be repaired and no garment carried or required a designer label. Cupboards were not stuffed with unwanted cooking utensils and there were a limited number of hand tools.

As a boy of five or six, I remember driving old rusty nails with a hammer that had a broken claw. It was a very old hammer at that time, but almost twenty years later it still was the only hammer about the house. Other tools were a pair of nippers and a spanner that was used on the plough. We called it a wrench. We owned a saw, a coarse rasp and two packing needles used for sewing bags of corn. We also had a gadget for twisting hay or straw rope. Brushes for sweeping the roads and the yard were always kept in good shape, as were the shovels for handling stones. We had a pitchfork and a long-shafted fork, two grapes[12], a couple of spades, a crowbar and a pick. A scythe, a shearing hook, a turf spade and a turf barrow more or less completed the range of tools.

As we lived quite close to the bog we usually had a good supply of turf, although the quality of some was poor. They were burned on the hearth fire. Here all the cooking utensils were of the heavy cast iron type and were old, yet in all of the eighteen years we lived in our Laragh home, I never knew of one to be damaged or replaced. There was a large twelve-gallon pot used to boil potatoes for the fowl and pigs. A slightly smaller one in which gruel was made for calves and a third one that was kept clean and used to boil the potatoes for our dinner. In the evenings it was used for making porridge for the supper and the breakfast. Bread was made in an oven, a flat-bottomed utensil with a flat lid, on which coals were placed when baking was in progress. Sometimes a small three-legged stand, which we called a 'crow', was used to place a saucepan on or near the fire. Coals were placed underneath to heat milk or cook some dainty dishes. Although frowned on by today's health experts, a large frying pan was a much used cooking appliance back then. Indeed, no vegetables, be they peas, beans, turnips, carrots or cabbage, tasted right until it was fried in the fat of the home cured bacon. Moreover, if butter was scarce in the wintertime, we often fried our bread in the bacon fat.

Seasons seemed to be far more pronounced back then. Long periods of hard frosty weather and regular heavy snowfalls were prevalent from early in November until the end of February. Cattle were housed during these months and required a lot of attention. Water was carried from the well in buckets to each animal, as a piped water supply was unheard of until many years later. At our house, corn was threshed in the barn and we tied the straw in bundles. In our neighbourhood, these bundles were called 'bottles' and they were easily carried when feeding the cattle. Work in the barn was carried out on wet days.

After the corn was threshed the grain was cleaned. This job was done with the barn-fan, a hand operated appliance that blew away the chaff and removed all the dirt and small seeds. When cleaned, a few sacks of the best quality grain were taken to the corn mill to be made into oat meal which was used for making porridge. A further quantity of good grain was kept for seed to be sown in the springtime.

Winter was also a time for cleaning sheughs, making drains and, in my father's case, keeping the roads clean. If the weather was favourable, ploughing could be done. The long dark nights were spent sitting around the fire. A couple of nights each week visitors, or as we called them 'céiliers', would drop in, usually before eight o'clock and they would stay until after ten. We had no electric light but my father could read the paper sitting close to the lamp and my mother seemed to have no trouble knitting in semi-darkness.

St. Patrick's Day on the 17th March was regarded as the beginning of spring. It was then time to sow the corn and plant the potatoes. Everything would have been prepared by that date. Twelve stone of seed corn was required for each acre of ground to be sown. A corn fiddle was used to spread the seed evenly and the sower had to maintain a steady speed. This was difficult on steep hills. A harrow, pulled by two horses, covered the seed. To do so properly the harrow had to pass over all of the ground five times. It was estimated that a farmer who harrowed a five-acre field in one day had walked twenty five miles on the rough ground.

Even more work was required to make the ground ready for potatoes. A greater depth of clay was needed to make the drills. While this work was being done the seed potatoes were being got ready, usually by the housewife. In days gone by potatoes were never planted whole. Each potato was cut in two or even three parts making sure that there was at least one 'eye' in every section. It was thought that one or two strong shoots or stems were better than several weaker ones. Dropping the potatoes by hand was slow and tiring work. It was also painful on one's back. Potatoes were placed in the drills about fifteen inches apart. Great pride was taken in making straight drills. Indeed it was a true measure of good horsemanship.

Even before the planting was completed, preparations were being made for the next job, the cutting of the turf. Mortises and the wheels of turf barrows and the head of the turf spade shaft were often dried up and loose after being kept in a dry place since last used. These were placed in deep water and weighted down for a couple of days. This caused the timber to swell and firm up the joints. It was endeavoured to have the turf cut before the end of May. At this time turnips and cabbage or kale were planted and the potato drills weeded and moulded (fresh clay put up around the green shoots).

Come June and the summer, it was now time to start the hay, weather permitting. When the grass was cut it was left to lie for a day. We then used forks to turn it over and if the weather was fine it was allowed to lie another day before being 'lapped'. Laps were the amount of hay one could lift in one's arms, roll it in a neat ball and set it out in rows. When in this position a shower of rain did it little harm. It was allowed to sit for about a week and was then built into what we called 'rucks'. The amount of hay in each ruck would compare with a small horse load. About three weeks later it was carted in and built in a huge "peak" in the haggard[13]. It was then thatched and securely tied with ropes. Used ploughshares were tied on the cross-ropes to keep them tight. It was built on a ring of stone. This we called a 'stile'. It had a diameter of about ten-feet and kept the hay up of the damp ground.

Hay making in good weather was a pleasure. The warm sun, the smell of the hay and plenty of help made work a joy. An effort was made to have the upland hay saved in June to be ready to start the meadows in July.

We knew meadows as low-lying damp fields on which hay was saved every year. They were seldom or never ploughed. In my earliest days some upland hay was allowed to grow a little longer until the seed was ripe. It was then cut and tied in sheaves. Later it was built in 'huts'[14]. After some time it was threshed and the seed was sold in the grass seed market.

On days unsuitable for haymaking we worked at the turf, spreading and clamping them. It was desirable to have the turf home and the hay in the haggard in early August. In days gone by it was quite normal for the previous year's crop of potatoes to last until the end of July. As children we spent many hours removing the buds of the old spuds. The digging of the first new spuds was something we looked forward to and soon it became a daily chore and a job for a man each morning before breakfast. Before long the faintest change of colour could be seen in the cornfields and we knew that the harvest was nigh.

I often heard it said that it was a poor sign of any work-man if he could not find a job on a good harvest day. So much depended on having help available when the corn was ripe and the weather fine. Two horses with a reaper could cut about five or six  acres of oats in a day but at least a dozen of able-bodied helpers were required to tie and shook the sheaves. Our family and two neighbouring families who were our cousins all worked together as a group.

To us harvest time was great fun.

On damp days, or whenever the morning dew had failed to lift, preparations were made for the stacking of the corn. Whins (gorse bushes) were cut to place underneath the stacks. They were arranged in circles, about seven or eight feet in diameter, and had a dual purpose. Firstly, they kept the sheaves of corn up off the damp ground, and secondly, they prevented rats or mice burrowing underneath the stacks. Props were required to prevent the stacks from toppling. These props were usually young ash trees, which grew in abundance in most hedgerows. Posts, six to seven feet long and about four inches in diameter were also suitable for props.

Even in fine weather it was necessary to allow the cut corn to remain in the stooks for at least two weeks before stacking would begin. Spare moments in late harvest time were spent cutting rushes to thatch the corn stacks. On a couple of occasions when I was still very young I remember helping to twist straw or hay rope to 'lap-rope' the thatched stacks of corn. Lap-roping meant walking round and round putting bands of rope, about eight inches apart, on the top of the thatched stack. Four cross-ropes over the top of this kept everything secure for the winter.

One last job remained to be done before winter set in. The potatoes had to be dug and made safe. The older people did not like to dig potatoes and put them in pits until October. They waited until the leaves had withered and all of the new potatoes got free from the roots of the old plant. Again when all was ready, a plentiful supply of help could get the work done in a short time but this not always possible as the schools would have reopened and young teenagers were classed as good potato gatherers. Often it was arranged to dig the potatoes on a Saturday and in the wartime the 'powers that be' agreed that all schools could take an extra week's holiday so that children could help with the potato gathering. Poor weather often foiled this arrangement.

## Youthful Days.

As I stand on the hilltop, what do I see,
Cows on the pasture, sheep on the lea,
Not one acre of tillage do I see at all,
No harvest to save when it comes to the fall.
How vast is the change since I was a lad,
And the view from this hilltop did make me feel glad,
When the valley was dotted with fields of ripe corn,
And the golden ears glistened with dew in the morn.

Golden cornfields in a patchwork of green,
In hues and in shades that are no longer seen,
Dark where the potatoes and turnips were sown,
Pale was the new grass where the meadow was mown.
Purple the heather that grew on the mountain,
Silver the stream that flowed from the fountain,
Yellow the rough ground where the whins did grow wild,
And the lark sang so sweetly when I was a child.

At the age of fourteen, it gave me no bother,
To drop the old school bag, for I was no scholar,
Soon I learned to dig spuds and to handle the spade,
And many a perch of stone drains I have made,
On a three-legged stool I could milk the cow,
Until I got promotion to handle the plough,
The horses were strong and the plough a great weight,
The neighbours would taunt if the furrows weren't straight.

When the ploughing was finished it was time to sow,
The corn it was scattered with fiddle and bow,
Some oldish neighbours, with a small bit of land,
Carried corn in an apron and sowed it by hand.
In April each year we worked long and steady,
Tilling the ground and getting spuds ready,

*If we did the work well the crop would be good,*
*The potato in those days was our staple food.*

*We prepared for the bog when the tillage was done,*
*And work in the bog was far from being fun,*
*The cutter was the man, who used the turf spade,*
*The filler then lifted the turf that were made,*
*Twenty-one turf and the barrow was full,*
*Twas the barrow-mans job to lift it and pull,*
*We worked a long day, from nine until seven,*
*Then we'd sometimes played football till nearly eleven.*

*A week after cutting, turf were turned on the ground,*
*We 'footed' or 'rickled' any dry one we found,*
*Every dry day we turned it about,*
*Then built it in 'clamps' to let it dry out.*
*There's still two more jobs to be done, we are told*
*There's stones to be gathered and corn to be rolled.*
*By then May was over, we were now into June,*
*The weather being fine we would start the hay soon.*

*While we were waiting on the cut grass to win,*
*There was potatoes to weed and turnips to thin,*
*A special job set out for every new day,*
*The peas needed rodding and the spuds needed spray.*
*There were walls to be whitewashed and old doors to paint,*
*In days long gone by old farmyards looked quaint,*
*With hay safe in the peak by mid July,*
*We'd hope that the turf in the bog would be dry.*

*It did not take long to cart home the peat,*
*But it took quite a while to build it up neat,*
*We used an abundance of turf long ago,*
*On cold winter nights with the frost and the snow,*
*And during the daytime mother used quite a lot,*

*Boiling potatoes in a ten-gallon pot,*
*Every day she baked bread in an oven back then,*
*Two massive big scones for a family of ten.*

*Saving the harvest was the job we loved best,*
*Even though for a time we got little rest,*
*Time did not seem to matter, if the weather was dry,*
*We worked every moment and time seemed to fly.*
*For man or for horse there was little relief,*
*As we cut and lifted and bound every sheaf.*
*Once harvest work started there was no time for slack,*
*Until the corn was all saved and built in a stack.*

*Now twas October but we still could not quit,*
*There were spuds to be dug and put in a pit,*
*Then covered with rushes and plenty of clay,*
*To protect them from frost on the cold winter's day.*
*There was a big plot of turnips that we had to sned,*
*Then cart them in quickly and put them in a shed,*
*We had threshing to do, cattle had to be fed,*
*Crushed oats on their turnips and straw for their bed.*

*We were ready for winter; most things were secured,*
*The fat pig was killed and the bacon was cured.*
*With a churn full of milk near the pantry door,*
*We churned the milk on Tuesdays, and had butter galore.*
*We had eggs every morning, straight from the ducks nest,*
*There were plenty of hen eggs, but we liked the ducks best.*
*Most foodstuffs we used then, we produced it ourselves,*
*Now sadly it's bought from the super mart shelves.*

# When the War Was Over

The farm on which we lived during the war years was small, about twenty five acres. Each year it was necessary to use land taken in conacre to grow oats which helped to supplement the winter feed for cattle. In 1944 my father decided to buy a larger farm. This he did in November of that year and we moved there in April 1945. As the new holding was only about three miles distant and in the same parish, thankfully we still had our old neighbours. While the dwelling house on the new farm was recently built and in good shape the out buildings were in need of much repair. A second horse was bought to help with the extra work.

The harvest of 1945 was difficult. Long periods of sultry weather caused the grain to sprout, and some had to be discarded. Nothing worthy of note took place in 1946 with the repairing of old farm buildings using up all spare time. Building materials were still very strictly rationed; only home-grown timber was available and it was recommended that asbestos roofing be used instead of corrugated iron. Late in the year a third horse was bought in anticipation for the amount of spring work that lay ahead.

But, the best laid plans of mice and men are thwarted every now and then. In mid-January 1947 a sharp frost set in and it was to last for over seven weeks. The ground was frozen to a great depth and the river was frozen over. The thick ice made it possible for us to walk for miles on the surface and a car was driven over a lough near to Dungannon. In February the heaviest snowfall in living memory swept the land. The snow drifted and many hollow places were filled to a depth of ten foot. In a number of places one could only guess where the road or the river ran. To clear a path on the main roads took almost a week and many of the smaller roads were still blocked a month later. On north-facing slopes some snow was to remain for over six weeks.

Many great stories were told about the depth of the snow in different places. One man told of how he was worried about the small amount of turf he had in his shed, so he cut the only few branches of a tree he could find. He then hung the saw on a small branch and carried the sticks home. Some weeks later when he needed the saw again he remembered using it to cut the branches and went to find it. After a long search he saw it hanging on the branch of a tree about eight feet from the ground! Another chap told of how he was trying to make his way to Sixmilecross. Only a few rooftops and the branches of an odd tree were showing above the snow. He noticed a little spot where the snow was dark coloured and he imagined he could see a little smoke coming up. He ventured towards the spot and kicked away some snow only to find a chimney. He bent down and asked, "Is there anyone in there?" A voice came back, "I'm here surely but I can't get out, sure the auld door's jammed." Not being too sure where he was, he asked, "Who am I talking to?" Quick and sharp the answer came back, "It's Hannah Mullin, who the hell do you think it is?" Her house was close to the road, but at a much lower level. Her doorway may have been blocked but I doubt if her chimney was covered.

## Snow

Just a few lines to fill up this space
To highlight the folly of the whole human race.
How the Mc's and the O's the Wards and the Owens
Are striving like mad to keep up with the Jones.

Now I'm not denying that there are people so smart
Who could replace your old hip or even your heart
They can travel through space, put a man on the moon
They send gadgets to mars and may land up there soon!

But last winter the forecasters warned us of deep snow
What gave them that notion I don't really know.
We were told that the snow might be up to our knees
And forewarned us of frost, minus umpteen degrees.

Twas rumoured the roadfolk spent millions on salt,
Afraid all the traffic would grind to a halt.
The gritters were filled and left at the ready,
And all drivers well warned to drive careful and steady.

Now when scarcity's mentioned, it's every man for himself,
Soon there wasn't a loaf left on the shop's shelf.
Gas tanks were topped up though none were quite empty
At the time of a storm we all like to have plenty.

Lorries were flying with oil for the fire.
The farmer was lagging the pipes in the byre.
The plumber was asked to mend pipes if they burst,
If anything happens we all want to be first.

But then as it happens, there wasn't a fall,
In fact, around here we had no snow at all.
Just wintry weather with the odd spit of rain
So the bathfull of water was let down the drain.

*The wains had been promised they would get out to ski*
*They whinged when they heard that it wasn't to be.*
*They were sure that the school would be closed for the week,*
*And when they get crabbit they would give you auld cheek.*

To return to the farm work, things were not running to our plan. It seems the newly purchased horse had recently become infected with a disease known as 'strangles' and he infected both our horses. They required veterinary attention but thankfully both were sufficiently recovered to be able to work when the weather improved. The remainder of 1947 and the busy part of 1948 seem to have passed without anything noteworthy taking place but it was discovered that the cost of keeping and caring for three horses far outweighed the cost of running a tractor. In November of 1948 two horses were sold and we bought a new David Brown tractor and plough for £345-0s-0d.

I got my first driver's licence at that time, at the age of 21. It was difficult to handle the tractor and plough and compete with the neatness of the horse work but thankfully the crops grew and yielded just as well.

Another year passed and another year's work was almost complete. It was the nineteenth of November 1949, Sixmilecross fair day. We still had the small farm where we had spent our childhood days. My father and I were over there doing some tidying up when a messenger came from the fair. He told us that an old neighbour, who was in fact a distant relation of ours, was in the fair and wished to sell his farm. He wanted to know if we would be interested. We chatted about the matter for a few moments and then my father got on his bike and went to Sixmilecross. I was in bed and asleep before he returned that night.

Next morning, when we were having our breakfast my father remarked, "Did you know that you bought a farm of land last night?" I hoped it was cheap. The cash in my pocket was a few coins, total value less than a fiver. However some time later the small farm on which we were reared was sold and the budget was balanced once again.

Although the area of new farm was more than double the size of the one we sold, it had many drawbacks. The land was impoverished and required a lot of drainage, the outbuildings were beyond repair and although the walls of the dwelling house were sound, the roof was in very poor condition. One could lie in bed and count the stars. We had the roof repaired immediately when the former owner vacated the house. In 1950 we laid a quarter of a mile of inch piping and got connected to the mains water supply. The yearly bill for a mains water supply at that time was £5 flat rate and it remained that way for a number of years.

1950 was spoken of as the Holy Year. It was also a very wet year and digging drains and cleaning sheughs was still spadework in those days. There were no mechanical or hydraulic diggers; at least, they were not available to do farm work. The stones of the old byres, stable and other old buildings were broken with a heavy sledgehammer and used to 'pipe' the drains. It took almost three years to clean up the fields. A 50% grant was available for such work at that time.

# Rashes and Remedies

*"Doctor, doctor, can I have a prescription please?"*

It would be interesting to know the name of the doctor who wrote the first prescription when the Health Service was introduced away back in 1948. It would be equally interesting to know just how many millions of prescriptions have been handed out since then. It's hard to believe that penicillin was still in short supply as it was one of the first drugs available. It was discovered in the early 1940s by Alexander Fleming and his Oxford colleagues E. Chain and H. Florey. They found that penicillium-notatum mould cured certain infections in animals. It was first used on humans in the army in 1943. Since then it has cured many ills and saved many lives.

I understand that a local man was one of a small group who played a part in the very first tests carried out in Northern Ireland. His name was William McFarland, late of Ballykeel, Sixmilecross. It seems he had an injury which was not responding to treatment. As a result he was sent up to a Belfast hospital. While there he was told that doctors were trying out a new drug and asked if he would volunteer to take part. He agreed and was moved into a small ward with a few other patients. Some days afterwards, a small man wearing an old brown hat walked into the ward, introduced himself and shook hands with each volunteer. He was none other than Mr. Alexander Fleming himself! In Mr. McFarland's case the drug was immediately successful and we know that William lived to a ripe old age.

Prior to the discovery of penicillin the range of drugs was very limited and their curative capability minimal. They were, for the most part, sulphur drugs. Sulphur was administered to man and beast alike. Saltpetre was also used in limited amounts.

Disinfectants, too, were of a basic nature. Iodine, Jeyes Fluid and washing soda was the most common. Anyone who complained of having a sore throat was in danger of having it painted with iodine. It was often applied on doctor's advice. Usually the first application did not sting too badly but each further painting became more painful as the skin dried and cracked. Another so-called cure for a bad throat was to fill ones socks with salt, and tie it around your neck at bedtime. I can assure you sleep did not come easily!

There was limited choice when buying soap back then. You took your pick, white or red. Lifebuoy was the brand name on the red soap. It was used for personal hygiene but one was well advised to keep the eyes tight closed, as it was extremely painful if it got inside. I'm not sure if there was a trade name on the white soap. It was in larger bars and was used on washdays. When all the clothes were washed there was usually a lot more than fitted on the clothesline. Those that remained were spread out on the hedge. When dry, it was necessary to keep the ones from the hedge apart as they required a good shake to remove the earwigs. As children we had great fun prancing on the insects as they landed on the ground. Detergents and sterilizing powders were unheard of at this time. Instead, all food vessels and cutlery were washed with, or dipped in boiling water. So too were the milking buckets and creamery cans. The churn, the wooden butter dish, the butter spades and the 'print' which were used for shaping the pats of butter, were sterilized with boiling water. This was known as 'scalding.' Other cleaning agents that I remember in those bygone days were, 'bath-brick', a small block about two inches square. It was used for cleaning tin or metal objects and was applied with a damp cloth. 'Vim' was also used, it may still be available. 'Oxadol' was one of the very early washing powders. There is a great wee story told about it which I have no doubt is true.

At that time a young couple lived in Beragh village. The man's name was Pat and his work meant that he was away from home quite a bit, occasionally overnight. After some time Pat made a remark and hinted that there must have been a party, as the grocery expenses seem high. The wise wife pretended not to hear but afterwards she kept a strict account of every penny she spent. Some time later a second remark was made referring to the housekeeping expenses and food cost. Again the good woman said nothing but presented Pat with the list she had kept. He looked down through it and commented. "I knew that there was 'fussies' being eaten here and I never get any." She asked him what he was referring to as fussies and he replied, "I see Oxadol marked down here in a couple of places and I never got any of it." "Oh," said she, "There is still some left in the house and you can have some right now." Whereupon she emptied some on a desert plate, put some milk on it, stuck a spoon in it and set it before him. Pat didn't sup much but he got the message. They lived happily ever after.

As chemical companies developed they, in conjunction with members of the Department of Agriculture, persuaded farmers to use specially manufactured detergents and sterilizers. Unfortunately the use, or perhaps the overuse, of these products was, in part, responsible for the world wide pollution problem we are experiencing today.

Once, when we were young, a bout of measles caused the school to be closed for some time. Three or four of our family were affected. I remember my mother pulling young nettles and washing the roots. She boiled them for quite a while, then strained off the liquid and made sure each of us drank a measured dose. I think we got a second helping later in the day. It must have had the desired effect, as we were all ready for school as soon as it reopened. Some time later a bout of mumps affected a large number of children in the area. For this complaint, a different therapy was recommended. To ensure a speedy and full recovery, each ailing youngster was encouraged to pass underneath a donkey. At the height of the outbreak we are told that there was a long queue at a house in Cloughfin where a quiet donkey had a 'practice'.

For those who were troubled with boils or had a blood disorder

Brainse Bhaile Thormod
Ballyfermot Library
Tel. 6269324/5

'bogbine' was supposed to be the cure. I understand it was treated in much the same way as the nettles. As bogbine only grows in certain areas, some local resident usually had the art of identifying the plant and preparing the medicine.

Personally, I would stop short of condemning all old time cures based on herbs or plants or things of that nature, but in many cases their preparation could only be described unhygienic.

Any married couple who had the same surname prior to their marriage was said to have a cure for the whooping cough. When a patient was brought to their home the couple were expected to give the ailing person three gifts. These gifts would be very small items, such as an apple, an orange and perhaps a biscuit. Any three small articles were supposed to suffice provided they were not similar. Nowadays immunisation of children, from when they are two months old until they have reached their fifteenth year, leaves little need for the old-time cures.

For the vast majority of lay people, it is difficult to understand the inability of the Health Service to provide adequate care for those in need. Almost all news bulletins tell us of long waiting lists and patients being left on trolleys in the corridors. I am aware and thankful to be in a position to state that I have never had to suffer such inconvenience. Yet while I have no wish to bore readers with 'my story', I believe it might go some way to highlight the difference between then and now.

During all of my teen years, and for a further eighteen, I was almost continually troubled with acne and boils. Different doctors tried and failed to make any lasting improvement and many who claimed to have 'the cure' were given a chance, but all to no avail.

In the summer of 1954 I sought the help of a skin specialist. He suggested plastic surgery. I was admitted to the Royal Hospital in Belfast in December for preparations and transferred to the Throne Hospital in the first days of the New Year. After the operation I was kept for about a month and had dressings changed each day. Thankfully the operation was a great success. The reason I am telling the story is to highlight the vast difference in the health service between then and now.

On the Sunday evening, just a few days before I was due to go home, the surgeon who performed the operation approached me. He explained how he had an operation planned for early next morning and he was not sure that the porter or butler would be in. He asked if need be, would I help him to carry a patient to the operating theatre. I agreed, but my assistance was not required, as the porter was at hand to help. I should explain that there did not seem to be any lift in the Throne Hospital and the theatre was up a flight of stairs.

The stretcher used was two long poles and a bit of canvas similar to the one used on a football field. On different occasions the surgeon helped to carry patients and, if need be, another able-bodied patient helped. Actually my stay in hospital was more than two months and during that time there was no mention of waiting lists or patients on trolleys. Nowadays one would expect to be on the waiting list for months, maybe years, and after the operation to be discharged in less than a week. So, why now the scarcity of beds and why the waiting lists?

# Pleasures and Pastimes

Pastimes, sport or indeed entertainment of any description played but a small part in our early teenage lives. Those were the war years and the rules were strict back then and easily enforced. The modes of travel were limited; Shank's mare or utility bikes being the most common forms of transport. Utility bikes were the cheapest possible type of bicycle. Made of poor quality steel, painted black and with no chrome, no gear changes or gear-case and with a poor quality saddle they most certainly were not built for comfort. All wartime material and equipment was of the utility class. Even some workers fell into this category and were expected to serve in any capacity when called upon. Utility, as described in the dictionary, made for usefulness or profitability rather than beauty.

In most of my teenage years we were all expected to let it be known where we were going and to be home before 10:30 or, by exemption, 11:00 at the latest. Even the Ancient Order of Hibernians Hall in Beragh was out-of-bounds unless on the odd occasion when it was loaned or rented for a school or parish concert. At their monthly meeting on the 4th of July 1942 the members of the Beragh Ancient Order of Hiberians Divison No.365 agreed to sell the hall to the then parish priest, the Rev. Alfred McKernan, for the reduced sum of £500. It was not until the 21st of July 1943 when all documents were signed and sealed that the keys were handed over. This led to a slight relaxing of the restrictions and we were allowed to go the Irish dancing classes, but eleven o'clock was still bedtime. On summer evenings we played football or handball. Handball was played at the upper gable of the hall.

Rabbits were very plentiful, in fact they were almost a plague in sandy soils or spots where they found it easy to make burrows. There was also a big demand for them. Food was very scarce in the cities and abroad so we spent much of our spare time hunting or setting snares. Not being professionals at either job we did little to lessen the rabbit population.

Winter nights, in the years after I left school, seemed very long as there was no electric light, and it was customary to be finished work and have the animals fed by five o'clock. When the evening meal was over, if no visitors were expected, my father would some-times repair boots which needed a patch or required a half-sole.

My mother busied herself at the sewing machine or at knitting as did my sisters, all of whom were older than I, bar one. I some-times tried my hand at fretwork and many an old plywood tea chest got torn apart as I endeavoured to turn waste timber into objects of beauty. Rarely did I succeed. We did have visitors, or céilíers as we called them, a couple of nights each week and we returned the call.

Sometime about the mid-forties the parish priest bought a three-quarter sized billiard or snooker table. It was a second-hand table and it was placed in an empty room of the old teacher's residence. This provided the youth and some older men with what we considered great entertainment in the winter nights. Considering that the room was only about fifteen-foot square and that included the stair landing, a player had little space when cueing. We played a game called skittles, with five little pegs standing near the centre or blue spot on the table. We used one red and two white balls. Each skittle had a different number and the winner had to finish with a score of twenty-one by playing a cannon type shot and knocking the correct skittle.

There was no limit to the amount of players who could take part. I've seen as many as twelve players take part in the same game, while, at the same time, shoved tight into a corner, were four older men enjoying a game of solo. Some men who had little interest in any of the games would call in for a chat. One particular man, whose quality of life was not improved by the company of his mother-in-law in his home, called in on a regular basis.

Murders were very rare back in those days but at this particular time a man was on trial in London for murdering his mother-in-law. Each evening the progress of the trial was debated in our clubroom. On the last day of the trial our visitor called in to the games-room and enquired if anyone had heard the result of the trial. Someone who had listened to the news spoke up and said the accused had been found guilty and had received the death sentence. There was silence for a little while before our friend replied. "Do you know", said he, "It's a shame, that poor man deserved a medal."

In the mid 1940s a new film projector was bought for use in the Parish hall. The make of the machine was a DeBree and it used 16mm film. A projector room was erected high above the door of the Hall. It is still to be seen there. Liam Kelly, who worked as a clerk in Sixmilecross Co-op, was employed to take charge in the projector room. Others were asked to give voluntary help. My assignment was to do doorman. Admission to the pictures was one shilling for adults, sixpence for children.

Two pictures were shown each week, one on Sunday night and a different one on Thursday. On many occasions all seats were filled and standing room only was the fate of all late comers. When exceptionally large crowds were expected it was sometimes found necessary to have a matinee on Saturday evenings prior to the night Sunday night's showing. At that time it was indeed strange to hear oldish men and women, who had spent most of their lives discussing the price of cattle or the condition of turf in the bog, now debating whither 'The Quiet Man' or' The Sound of Music' was the better film. For quite a while the pictures in the Hall were part of nearly every conversation in the district.

Another true story is told about a remark made by the late Mickey Hackett. Mickey wasn't a tall man and his wife Maggie was smaller. Even when the saddle of her bike was at its lowest Maggie had to rock from side to side to reach the pedals. The couple did not have a family. As the years rolled by Mickey thought a car would be very useful so he purchased an old Austin 7. As the couple were on their way to town one day Mickey stopped the car to chat to a neighbour who congratulated them on their new automobile. Mickey commented that the car was worth the money, but Maggie spoke up. "Ach, I don't know, sure maybe the 'wheen' [15] of pounds would have been better spent buying a couple of stirks [16]." "Arrah, sure woman would you hold your tongue," says Mickey "wouldn't the people get a quare laugh at you and me going down to the pictures in Beragh riding two stirks"[16].

BRIAN COLL and The BUCKAROOS

NEW RELEASE
A SIDE: THE SOLDIERS LAST LETTER
B SIDE: DIRT IN MY FACE

For more than ten years the support for the pictures in the hall continued but finally gave way as the craze for show bands and whist drives spread. From the mid forties and for the next ten years, drama, pantomime and talent contests provided great entertainment for many of us. A trip on the cheap excursion train to Bundoran on a fine Sunday evening was a novelty away back in the 1940s and on one occasion I remember a full-day bus trip to the Glens of Antrim and along the coast road. I think the fee was one pound, and that included a meal.

**MELODY ACES**

Sports days in the different areas created great interest in the summer months. These took quite a time to arrange and their success or failure depended to a big extent on weather conditions on the day of the event. I think it is worth noting that in those days few, if any, sports or football clubs had a sports or football field that they could call their own. It was common to see sports days advertised in a field kindly loaned by Mr X. The following year, sports held in the same area might well be held in a different field. This was because tillage was done each year on a rotating basis and the field where the sports were held might well be ploughed up the following year. In our area I remember sports events being held in different fields and on different farms. As a matter of fact I attended sports events in a field on our farm in the time of the previous owner. It is hard to believe that cyclists could and did compete in championship events on such ground.

# When Lightning Strikes.

The warm and sunny weather at the end of May and the first week of June this year (2007) brought back memories of many glorious summers in my lifetime. So too did the thunder storm and torrential rain which struck with little warning on the twelfth day of June causing flooding and disaster in many towns and villages. Strangely enough, storms of wind, rain, or snow seem to act in some way like milestones as we look back over the years.

My father so often spoke of a windstorm that struck on the 29th January 1927. Maybe it was because a cousin of mine was born on that same night or more likely the fact that a lot of very large trees were blown down on a neighbour's farm and he got a considerable amount of useful timber. The morning after the storm all the damage it caused was covered by a fall of snow.

It seemed that several of the trees fell across the laneway and it was necessary to have it cleared quickly. The quality of the timber was considered very suitable for making cart wheels especially the felloes (the outer rim) and the hubs or naves (the centre parts). My father took suitable lengths of this timber to a sawmill near Gortin where there were machines capable of turning and cutting out the naves and felloes. A local carpenter, John Kelly, made the wheels and the body of the cart and Mick McMackin, the blacksmith, put the iron hoops on the wheels.

Twenty two years later, on the 19th of November, my father was a sad man when he allowed me to take the wheels off the cart, cut off the shafts and put on small 'aeroplane wheels' so as to make the cart into a small trailer for the tractor.

On the twelfth of July 1932, the worst thunderstorm that I, and indeed many others, can remember, struck in the afternoon. It was a sweltering hot and sultry day after a long period of glorious summer weather. As we made our way home from school we could hear the faint rumble of thunder away in the distance. My sisters tried to hurry me along but the heat was overpowering. We had just arrived home and had our dinner taken when a big black cloud appeared on the horizon and the noise of the thunder grew louder. My mother was alone in the house with two children younger than I was. My father, my older sister and a workman were at our cousin's farm helping with the hay.

Soon the black cloud was almost overhead and we could see the odd flash of lightning before we felt the first drops of rain. They were great big heavy drops and ice cold. As the ferocity of the storm increased the noise of the rain on the corrugated iron roof of a nearby shed was deafening and although it was only about five o'clock it was quite dark. The rain turned to hailstones, some like lumps of ice and the lightning flashed almost continuously. It was well over an hour before there was any lessening of the thunder and lightning and much longer before there was any easing of the rain.

When we did venture out we could hardly believe what we saw. The scene outside was incredible. Large pools of water lay where dust had gathered a couple of hours earlier and summer garments looked a sorry sight, lying where they had been discarded in the heat of the day. Prior to the storm the little stream that ran close to our home was almost dried up. The same little stream was now a raging torrent being further supplemented by dozens of muddy streams gushing in from all directions.

In fact at that time it was common practice to leave broody hens standing in the water and place a big box over them. Then as they could not sit down they very soon lost their broody instincts and returned to laying. As it happened two or three had been put in the box that morning and no one remembered to let them out before the rain started. We were never to know if the hens had escaped. The box was never found.

In the potato field great heaps of clay lay at the bottom of the field where the rain had deposited it after carrying it down the hill. In the field much of the oat crop had been flattened.

Heavy falls of snow and long periods of frost were accepted as normal in days gone by, but the seven weeks of hard frost and deep snow in 1947 must surely hold the record. The frost came in the first days of February and the snow about two weeks later. Some roads were impassable for over a month. On St. Patrick's Day, the 17th of March, we still had lots of snow in sheltered places.

Thunder and lightning storms were common in the years that followed and almost went unnoticed. Not so with one that struck about 3pm on Sunday, 5th June 1960. Early in the afternoon quite a few wicked flashes of lightning and loud brattles of thunder disturbed the calm of what had been a pleasant day. When the storm had passed over the sun reappeared and the evening seemed fine. Unfortunately what seemed to be was not so. When my father went to bring in the cows for milking five of his seven cows lay dead, the other two were standing chewing their cud. The five that were dead were lying in comfortable positions, just as if they were asleep. They were spread over quite a sizeable patch of ground, no two cows were touching each other and some were twelve to fifteen feet apart. They were a good distance from any hedge and there were no trees nearby. No cow had marks of any description.

Also, on the 4th September in the early 1960s we had gale force winds that destroyed the barley crop. It struck just as the crop was ripe and the heavy heads were easily broken off. The storm also toppled trees, damaged roofs and scattered newly built ricks of hay, we called them 'peaks' of hay. A neighbouring farmer, the late John McNamee, who lived on a very exposed farm, had all his hay scattered. As he went into the village next day a retired schoolteacher inquired if he had had any damage done by the storm. Johnnie replied that his peaks of hay were all tossed. "You're lucky" said the teacher, "I lost my new hat!"

# Energy

Years ago when I looked at the pictures in the schoolbooks, I often wondered why it was only Dutch people who made use of the windmills. Now, seventy years later, windmills are a common sight in our own country. For the most part they are used to generate electricity and, so far, they in no way impair the beauty of the countryside. But one could hardly be blamed if they questioned the efficiency of the system. One wonders just how many windmills would be required to fully supply the present day demand for electricity in the country. Perhaps it might be just a few too many.

Scarcely a day passes without the question of renewable energy arising. Maybe we should check just how wisely we use all the energy we consume? It may sound ridiculous, but prior to 1940, at least 95% of all energy was renewed by a good night's sleep and a hefty breakfast. This applied to man and horse alike. Remember, there were no mechanically powered machines, and although electricity had reached the towns and villages, it was not affordable in country areas for a good few years.

In the not so distant past, the selling of coal was big business in towns and villages but with the advent of central heating, fuelled by oil or gas, sales of coal have dwindled significantly. So too has the cutting of turf. Someone rightly said, "Turf were great things. They warmed you at least three times. Once when you are cutting them, again when you pack them up in the shed and a third time when they burn on the fire."

There is no doubt that a lot of sweat was lost cutting the turf. I can well remember, as a young boy, feeling the drops of sweat fall on my hands from the brow of the man who was cutting the turf as I lifted them and placed them on the barrows. The man who pulled the barrows also lost a lot of sweat. Oodles of sweat and energy were lost in the hayfields and in the haysheds too.

Today it would be unusual to see someone sweating at work. Pushing buttons, pulling levers or turning a steering wheel accomplishes most jobs. Even an egg can be whisked or one's teeth cleaned without having to make an effort to flick a wrist. Spades and shovels are now things that two or three men lean on while they watch a hydraulic machine digging a hole! But while we shy from shedding a drop of sweat or an ounce of energy at work, we seem to have no qualms about driving ourselves to the limit in the gym or on the sports field. And most likely, if the gym is two hundred yards from our home, we will use the car to get there!

To be honest I know little about gyms, but sometimes curiosity gets the better of me and I do squint over the 'ads' in the bundles of junk that arrives in the letter box. It's surprising the number of apparatuses that are available for use in the home or the gym to help one exercise or lose weight. I noticed that quite a few required to be plugged into electricity to set them going.

The one that intrigued me most was the runner treadmill. You get on, start it up, run like 'billio' and go nowhere. It reminds me of the hamster in its exercise wheel. Then there is the tread climber. It counts your steps and the calories you burn. It also plays a wee tune and has a fan to make sure you don't overheat. There is a big variety, all shapes, sizes and prices. You could pay £3000 for one of them and get 21p change. Most of these gadgets require electricity to function properly, but the extraordinary thing is that with simple redesigning, all of them would generate electricity when being used.

Over seventy years ago we rode bicycles fitted with dynamos which generated sufficient light for travelling on the darkest nights. The first type of dynamo was fitted at the rear wheel and was rotated by the tyre, but in 1934 hub dynamos were fitted in the front wheel of many new bicycles. The extra energy required to pedal the bike when the dynamo was in action was unnoticeable, and most journeys included some up hill travel. There is little doubt that if all wasted energy could be converted into joules of power the savings would be significant.

In the early 1940s, no house or home in this district had a mains water supply. This meant that over 95% of all homes had no bathroom or indoor toilet facilities. A hot and cold water supply was something that only the very well off could hope to afford. There were no washing machines, dishwashers, tumble driers, vacuum cleaners or any electrical gadgets. Again, most houses still depended on hearth fires, while a very few had acquired stoves or ranges some of which had side-boilers. Central heating, as we know it today, was unheard of at that time.

Even the shops were different back then. Few commodities arrived pre-packed and there was no self-service. A trainee to the grocery trade was apt to spend the first year of their apprenticeship at the scales or weighbridge measuring pounds and half-pounds of tea, and stones (14 lbs), half-stones and quarter-stones of sugar, salt and flour. Most items were kept on shelves behind the counter, well out of range of the customers. There was usually a section of small drawers in some convenient spot where soda, cream of tartar, sulphur, saltpetre and such commodities were safely stored. A large pail of milk, a pint measure and a half-pint measure sat on one end of the counter. Each morning customers who required milk brought along small tin cans which held two pints, and the requested amount was measured in.

Credit was available to most shoppers but plastic cards or calculators were still unheard off. Nevertheless the speed and accuracy of totting up long lists of figures would astound many of today's young shoppers.

Referring back to the ten stone poke of flour, the sack or bag was always referred to as a poke bag. It was made from a white cotton material, possibly calico or percale. When empty they were washed and bleached and made into sheets for the beds. Four poke bags made a sheet for a double bed. The bleaching consisted of boiling them in water with a good measure of washing soda or caustic soda. Next they were spread out on longish grass for a couple of weeks in the hope that they would get a good nights frost. They were then sewn together and hemmed before being thoroughly washed and put into use. In some cases, where attention to detail was not strictly observed, the brand name of the flour maker could be clearly seen on sheets hanging on lines. One name seemed quite appropriate; it read 'Early Riser' and showed a rooster standing crowing.

No job was accomplished without the use of manpower or human energy. Women too played their part, often far beyond the call of duty, be it in the bog, the hay field or the harvest, or in the yard - milking the cows, feeding cattle, pigs and hens. Then, when the day was done and others rested, there was sewing, knitting, patching and darning to be done. And there were children to be seen to.


## A Mother's Touch

*A mother's work is never done*
*She's busy night and day,*
*Cooking, cleaning, washing*
*And drying tears away.*
*Caring for little children*
*Can be a constant toil,*
*Always one in need of help*
*Or a timid one to spoil.*

*Days and years pass quickly*
*Soon it's time for school,*
*Often not a happy day,*
*Tearful as a rule.*
*Even for a little while*
*It really seems unfair,*
*To leave your greatest treasure*
*In another person's care.*

*Then it's someone's birthday*
*Or a child has lost a tooth,*
*And all too quickly you're aware*
*That your eldest son's a youth,*
*In this world of pleasure seeking*
*Young folk are led astray,*
*With endless love and patience*
*You must try to show the way,*

*And the task is never easy*
*There is hardly time to rest,*
*Sometimes you will feel you have failed*
*When you've done your very best.*
*Just try and keep on praying*
*And great things will be unfurled,*
*When a gentle mother's hand*
*Is allowed to rule the world.*

If there was a very young family, the mother might have a young hired girl to give a hand, and most farmers had the help of a servant boy. On farms, horses were used to pull the plough, the harrow and some other few implements but all other work was done by manpower. All hand tools were used; spades, shovels, scythes, grapes, forks, pickaxes and sledgehammers.

In those days each house, even those in villages, had their own vegetable garden and the owner or tenant would proudly invite visitors on a guided tour. There was great rivalry to see whose potatoes would first sprout through the clay in the springtime or in whose garden the first blossoms would appear. Even the stationmaster at the railway and some of the porters used the railway slopes as gardens. Plots of vegetables could be seen, sometimes quite a distance from the station. The railway itself is a fine example of what can be achieved by manpower. On a quarter mile stretch of railway, visible from our yard, we could see the station house, the signals and four bridges. Three of these bridges were to accommodate roadways. The fourth was over the river. All railway bridges were stone built, each stone being specially chiselled to fit a special place. A nearby stretch of line ran through deep bog land. When this section was being laid, local men were paid to cut and supply furze or whins to lay on the bog. This layer of whins was then covered with stones on which the sleepers were laid.

*Beragh Bridge and Station House*

An old lady, Miss Johnston, told me that her great uncles, as young boys, had helped when the whins were being cut. More than one hundred years later, when the line was closed down and was being lifted by her brothers, they found the branches of the old whins still buried in the bog and quite sound.

For the most part, railways ran on low-level ground, often following the course of rivers. Sometimes this was not possible and great cuttings or gaps had to be hewn through hills and mountains, often through solid rock. In a few places we find tunnels. Considering that in Ireland over a thousand miles of track were laid, it is impossible to fathom the enormity of the task undertaken by men with primitive tools.

Furthermore, we use our roads daily and, other than to complain about the quality of the surface, we give little thought as to how the road came to be here at all. We do know that for the past sixty years council workmen have taken care of the roads' surface. Prior to that all of the tens of thousands of miles of Irish roads were made and repaired by local men, with the help of a horse and a few hand held tools.

If we still need proof of the bewildering achievements of bygone days, let us look at the steeples on some of our churches and cathedrals. The craftsmanship, patience, nerve and manpower required to erect these spires must surely convince all of us that our forebearers were highly skilled builders and hard working people. Although these examples of genius may have been accomplished more than a century ago, there was little or no change in the methods of work until the mid or late 1930s. It was then that electricity became available, and oil and engines were used to generate power.

About this time dramatic changes took place that revitalised all work methods and the outlook of most people. Six-month hiring contracts were abandoned and weekly paydays were introduced. So too were insurance cards, which were required to be stamped each week.

Steady work and a good weekly wage attracted many young men to jobs in factories in England. Young unmarried women were also tempted to go abroad in search of brighter futures. The departure of so many young workers and the demand for extra tillage made change inevitable. To abandon the old system that had served so well for generations was painful for old and middle aged farmers. To sell the horses and buy a tractor was unthinkable. However, change did come, slowly at first, but as the demand for home-grown foodstuffs became more compelling, a greater number of small grey tractors appeared on local farms.

Farming methods were not alone in being obliged to undergo change. In fact every aspect of life was to be transformed in one way or another. In the forge the electric welder took over from the

fire, the bellows, the anvil and the heavy hammer. Then, when an electric drill and grinder were installed, the forge became a workshop and the blacksmith, an engineer.

So too with the carpenter and the introduction of the electric circular saw, plane and the mortising machine. His workplace became the joinery and the carpenter became a joiner. Even the three foot long wooden measure or rule, that he folded and put in its special pocket on the right leg of his bib-and-brace overalls, was exchanged for a modern steel tape.

Horse drawn bread carts and traps gradually gave way to motorised vehicles and young ladies had their hair permed and wore headscarves. Still, change was slow and in some aspects of work it took quite a few years to make any great significance. While small grey tractors played a big part in speeding up tillage and haulage work, digging drains and trenches was still spade and shovel work for another fifteen or twenty years.

In 1939 a gang of workmen armed only with hand tools, dug and removed the soil and earth from a ten-foot deep hole for a reservoir near to Bernish Glen. They constructed the reservoir and dug a four-mile stretch of trench in which they laid the pipe, which provided the inhabitants of Sixmilecross village with a much needed supply of water. The only power or engine driven pieces of equipment used on this job were water pumps which kept the site of the reservoir free of water while the construction work was taking place. As it required a number of pumps working constantly to keep the area free of water, a night watchman was employed. He was the son of the plumber, a lad in his late teens whose heart had recently received a direct hit from one of cupid's arrows. On the night in question, the apple of his eye was attending a function in the village hall. Anxious about her safety, the young man decided to leave his post and escort her home. Understandably this assignment took longer than was originally planned. When he returned to the reservoir, all the pumps had stopped and were submerged in water, leaving the lovesick youth little choice but to wake his sleeping father and take the consequence. All night they toiled without success and next day larger pumps had to be hired in to clear the water off the site.

Here again disaster nearly struck. The extra volume and force of water from the big pumps caused the flow to take a different course and, but for the quick thinking of the site foreman, two dwelling houses downstream would have been flooded. But like the fairytale, this story has a happy ending. The love affair stood the test of time and some years later the young couple wed and lived happily ever after.

Over ten years later, another gang of men started in Sixmilecross and dug a deep trench along the roadside through Beragh village and continued until they reached the Omagh to Ballygawley road. They also laid the pipe and refilled the trench, which was over three miles long and about four to five feet deep.

Up until the early 1950s, mixed farming was the norm on the majority of holdings and fields were tilled in rotation every four or five years. Prior to ploughing a lea or grass field, the surrounding hedges were cut down or severely trimmed by the farm hand. There were two reasons for doing this. First, the crops did not yield well in the shelter of a big hedge and secondly, it allowed the horses and the plough to get closer to the fences so that little ground was wasted. Cutting hedges meant using a hedge-knife or a billhook, sometimes a handsaw was used. Two men using a crosscut-saw were required to cut larger trees. Hedges along the roads or laneways were trimmed annually with hand operated hedge-clippers. There were no power-operated tools.

In some places water driven wheels did create power to turn the millstones that ground the corn. They also drove the machines that scotched the flax. Scotching meant removing the hard outer shell from the stalk or stem of the flax and leaving the inner fibbers, which were made into linen. There were ten or twelve such water wheels in the district in my young days. About four miles away in the town land of Drumnakilly, a water wheel was used at a forge to drive a very heavy sledgehammer. I understand the McAleer family used it, mostly in the manufacture of spades.

Returning to the question of renewable energy, perhaps by placing new and more efficient water wheels at suitable places along the rivers and streams, meaningful amounts of power could be produced. But since electricity (alternating current) cannot be stored, the to-and-fro-ing of the tide on our Atlantic coast may be the most reliable source of renewable energy. Perhaps it would be worthwhile reflecting on how wisely we use our present supply. For a start, is all our journeys or travelling really necessary? One wonders where the big lorries get their loads and at the amount of cars with just a lone driver.

Considering that most workers now use a car or some type of vehicle to get to work, it would be interesting to know just how much fuel is used even before work begins. It is also accepted as a fact that quite a percentage of workers travel over fifty miles to work each morning. Furthermore, it is not uncommon for those travelling to work to meet others who ply the same trade travelling in a different direction.

Few of us who drive can claim never to have made an error of judgement, nor could we be justified in exposing flaws in another person's driving, but I can't resist commenting on one incident which really amused me. It happened about a year ago when I was being driven to Luton Airport after visiting my daughter and her family in London. It was an early morning flight and traffic was moving at about fifty miles as we neared the airport. Traffic on the left-hand lane was travelling slightly faster and a canary coloured Volkswagen Beetle type car drew up alongside our car. A lone young lady was driving. She had both hands on the steering wheel but in her right hand she also held an ordinary desert spoon. In her left hand she managed to hold quite a large round carton. I have no idea what the carton contained but she managed to scoff two or three spoonfuls as she sped past our car. It's most unlikely it was porridge.

One of the old men I enjoyed chatting with away back in the 1940s was a retired coalminer. His proper name was John Kerr but was better known as "the Bung-ga-rye." I tried to find how he managed to get this title but failed. Someone suggested it was the name of a song that Johnnie always sang if he got a drop of the "real owle mountain dew." Be that as it may, Johnnie still maintained he spent thirty years in the coalmines in Scotland. His favourite statement was "By Heaventers, for thirty years I barely saw the light of day. It was dark when we went down the shaft and it was dark when we got up again." It is uncertain just when he went to Scotland but he returned in the early 1940s.

He told of lying on his side working with a pick in shallow veins of coal more than one hundred feet below the surface. Some of the veins of coal were scarcely two feet in depth and he often had to lie in inches of water. In the pit where Johnnie worked, men were not paid by the day or the week, but by the weight of good coal, which they mined. Each man was given a trolley and a small sled with a length of rope attached to each end. He crawled to the coalface and raised enough coal to fill the sled. He employed a young boy to drag out the full sled and put the coal in the trolley while he raised more coal. The miner then used his rope to drag the sled back to the low coalface and refill it. When the trolley was full, it was taken to the surface where the coal was graded, weighed and the miners wages determined accordingly.

In later years I had the pleasure of visiting Lochgelly which is in the centre of Scotland's coal mining district, but only a few pits were in operation and these were worked by machines. Today I understand all pits in that area are closed. The machines lie abandoned in flooded mines and men like John Kerr are long since forgotten.

## Now and Then

How can I, in simple words, portray the things I see?
And not feel grieved when I recall just how it used to be,
When nature's pace was rule of thumb for all of God's creation.
And we had time for work and sleep and some for recreation.

When babes were taught how to behave well, sheltered from all dangers,
And old folk were nursed in their own home, not left in care of strangers.
Long gone the day when children small could safely walk to school
And we who trod it bare foot did face no ridicule.

Those were the happy carefree days, though worldly goods were scant
But neighbour shared with neighbour, no one was seen to want
The feilds were like a patchwork quilt, well tilled with horse and plough
The spade that cut the turf back then brought sweat drops from our brow

The summer time was pleasant then, and by the longest day
The air was sweetly perfumed by the smell of new-mown hay.
Later in the harvest time, in the early morn
We would see the dewdrops glitter on the golden fields of corn

Soon we'd hear the thresher's hum as it removed the grain
To winter feed the cattle or to sow in spring again.
The only oil we used back then was to keep the lamp aglow,
And the hearth fire kept us warm at night when we had frost and snow.

There were hens around the barn door, so we had eggs to sell
And four cows' milk to the creamery brought in some cash as well.
When the sow produced a litter someone had to sit all night
To see that they were feeding and make sure they did not fight.

In the spring it was lovely when the horses ploughed the lea
We would watch the flocks of white gulls come inland from the sea.
Some would land beside the plough SHARE, while others on the wing,
Could scoop a worm and stretch it like a piece of elastic string.

But now it's sixty years or more since we were ten years old,
And the changes that we've witnessed could not have been foretold.
Now take the little baby, whose arrival causes mirth,
It may find itself in day-care shortly after birth.

Then it may go to playschool or perhaps a nursery
I'm told that they are welcome there just as soon as they are three.
Then it's onto primary school and the eleven plus
That's the exam that's dreaded most and causing all the fuss

Next it's onto secondary school but if you don't make the grade
You might as well give up the books and find yourself a trade
Some go on to university and hope for a degree
But few can now afford it, so costly is the fee.

Forget about the farming, it really is a mess
What's going to happen to it is anybody's guess
You have to send a birthday card when every calf is born
And give the date and time of birth be it night or early morn.

You punch a tag in both its ears and record the dam's number
You log its colour and its sex before going back to slumber.
I drove from Beragh to Cork just the other day
And scarce a bit of tillage did I see along the way
Fields of grass for silage, but no potatoes, veg or wheat.
Its looks as if we now import the things we eat.

Now big tractors turn the soil, ten acre in a day
And scarce a worm that you will find now, wriggling in the clay,
No more the white gulls seem to come nor swallows soar on high,
Because modern farming methods harm the earthworm and the fly.

# Oh To Have A Little House.

Away back in the early 1950s a grant of four hundred pounds was available for the repair of a farm dwelling house. I made an application and, after the existing building was inspected, I received correspondence informing me that the house qualified for a grant. The next step was to submit two sets of plans and specifications to the County Council in Omagh outlining the repair work to be done and the proposed site for the septic tank. It was recommended that provision of a bathroom and toilet be included in the improvements. Few country houses had such facilities at that time.

Now, there is an old saying I am sure some of you have heard. It ran, 'it's hard to whistle if you have no lower lip'. It meant that it was difficult to pay if money was scarce. Mine was scarce and paying an architect to draw up plans just didn't make any sense. To be honest I had never seen a set of plans drawn by an architect. Someone told me that a rough sketch of the house and details of the work to be done were all that was required. Now, I had often seen sketches of byres and sheds drawn by Ministry personnel and I had no doubt that I was well capable of measuring the house and drawing up a document that would be sufficient to get me permission to start work. By this time I knew all the measurements of the house off by heart and at night-time I would sit and draw and write until at last I was satisfied that I had managed to produce a presentable copy.

Next morning I cycled to the County Council offices in Omagh. As I made my way up the corridor, unsure of where I was going, I met an elderly man who seemed to view me with suspicion. He was not the kind of person I had hoped to meet but when he enquired what my business was, I had little choice but to tell him. When I told him, he took the big envelope from me and there and then he opened it and took out the contents. He gazed at it for a couple of seconds, then turned it upside down and looked at it again. He then lowered it a bit and looked over the top at me as if I had two heads. "What is it?" he asked. I tried to explain but he unceremoniously pushed it towards me and ordered me to go and get a proper set of plans drawn.

That night I was telling some of my pals what had happened and one of them commented, "You must have met Mr. Glasgow, you were unlucky." I don't know who I met but I was downhearted. Downhearted, but not beaten. I knew a girl in Beragh village who was going out with a young chap that worked in the council office. I told her my predicament and gave her the sketches or plans. A short time later I had them back, all stamped and ready for use!

The approved work included the replacement of all windows and doors, plus plumbing and replastering of the entire building. All upstairs floors were also to be replaced. Most of the work was undertaken by myself and my brothers, with qualified tradesmen called on to carry out the plumbing and final coat of plaster. A qualified bricklayer was also employed to build the new chimneys.

In the winter of that year we had a very cold spell of weather. I remember being on a makeshift scaffold working at the house. I was only three or four feet from the ground when a plank gave way and I toppled to the ground and broke my collar bone. It was painful for a time but back in those days jobs could be found for anyone who had one sound arm. The broken bone healed quickly however. Progress on the house was slow that year as heavy frost interfered with all building and plastering work.

Prices of building materials and house fittings have changed considerably since 1955. I retained all documents and receipts and quote a few prices as they were half a century ago:

*Enamelled, oatmeal coloured solid fuelled cooker, with left-hand oven and back boiler, £36-10s-0d. Carriage on same, £2-10s-1d.*

*One white bathroom suite, (bath, wash-hand basin and toilet) complete with all fittings, £42-7s-0d.*

*Two tons of cement (delivered), £13-10s –0d.*

Overall, the work took about 6 months to complete and when all bills were settled and tradesmen paid, I still had some money left from the £400 grant that I had received. Try and compete with that at present day prices!

# To Have and to Hold

Work was still in progress at the dwelling house in the spring of 1955 when a chance meeting with a young county Cork lady meant that life took on a whole new meaning. It's difficult to imagine how, in one short week, work that had hitherto been a toil was now transformed into a labour of love.

Mary Aherne was a student mid-wife in Stophill Hospital in Glasgow when we first met. She had accompanied a cousin of mine, Mary McCartan, who was also a student mid-wife, on a short break home at Easter Time.

I first saw her at Mass time and wished that I had had an opportunity to speak to her. By making some discrete enquiries I learned that a group had arranged to go to a céilí dance in Omagh that night. My usual Sunday night entertainment or job was doing doorman at the pictures in the parochial hall and eyebrows were raised when I asked to be excused. I got a lift to the INF hall in Omagh where Mary and myself had several dances together. The two girls were due to return to Scotland the next day but were encouraged to stay an extra week. When they finally returned the matron threatened them with dismissal, thankfully they were relieved to get off with just a caution.

We kept in touch by letter and by phone. Stamps cost two and a half pennies or one penny in present day money. Phone calls cost six old pennies and if calls were made at night time it was seldom that we were asked to put in more money or were ever cut off.

My first visit to Cork was in early November 1955. It was on the occasion of Mary's elder sister's marriage. The journey was by train. Mary had travelled from Scotland to Belfast where she boarded the train for Dublin. I had taken an earlier train from Beragh and joined her at Portadown station. We arrived in Dublin at Amiens Street station and made our way across the city to Kingsbridge Station. We had a further change at Limerick Junction before we arrived at Mallow. From there a taxi took us the last twenty miles to our destination at Knockavilling, Lismire.

It was difficult to distinguish between family, neighbours and friends, as the house was full to overflowing. While it was difficult to understand the southern accent in the unfamiliar surroundings there was no doubting the genuineness of the welcome extended. The couple were wed the next day and things had still not fully returned to normal by the end of my three day visit. The first stage of my lone homeward trip was by pony and trap to Kanturk station on a frosty morning. From there the train journey was long, lonely and boring.

We were married in mid July 1956 and after a few days in Dublin returned to our newly renovated but sparsely furnished home in Deroar. About a year later we had a visit from Mary's uncle, Fr. Finbarr. He was the priest who had baptised her when she was a few days old. A few years later he had joined the Franciscan Order and had been in America for twenty years. When Mary met him at the door his first words were, "Oh my, how you have changed!"

He had flown to Scotland to visit his sister who was a retired teacher and together they had arrived at our house on their way to Cork. Now, I had six or seven years practice driving the tractor but had never driven a car. I had a driver's licence and at that time no one was required to pass a driving test so I decided to hire a car and drive to Cork.

I contacted the late John Grugan in Omagh and he agreed to have a car ready the following morning. I went down early next day, paid the money, collected some documents and the keys, and was shown the car. It was an old Morris 8. It had covered a lot of miles but I was anxious to get driving and did not complain. The engine started immediately when I turned the key but the car refused to go backwards. The gear positions were clearly marked on top of the gear lever but no effort on my part would get the lever into that position. Still not willing to give in I got one leg out and pushed

the car back just enough to get clear of the object that was in my way. Now I was able to get in and drive off. As I turned onto the roadway I glanced back and noticed a couple of mechanics staring in my direction, but, I had a place to go and, reverse or no reverse, I was going to get there.

When I reached home I was again in trouble. Luckily there was a slight slope in our yard and, by allowing the car to run back a couple of times I managed to get it turned. After we had a cup of tea we set off on our two hundred and forty-mile journey. Fr. Finbarr occupied the front passenger seat and in the back we had a couple of map-readers.

During the journey Fr. Finbarr recounted various tales of his twenty year mission in the New World, where most of his time was devoted to researching the history of the Franciscan Order in North and South America. Of all the stories he related the one that most often comes to mind is of a people he encountered whose philosophy on life was to never rest until they were assured that their neighbour was well and had sufficient for the day. Three large volumes of his work still remain in our house in Deroar.

After a couple of hours driving when we stopped for a meal, I made sure to choose a spot where I would not be blocked in. We stopped again when we had covered about two thirds of our journey. When we returned to the car this time I thought I would put on the lights to make sure they were working. Everything seemed grand, even the dashboard lit up, and there, staring me in the eyes, was another diagram of the gear positions, different to the one that was on the gear stick. The priest didn't bat an eye at what I uttered, but there was a comment from the rear seat. Someone had changed the little knob on top of the gear lever. I never did find out if it was done out of necessity or for devilment. Anyhow I returned from Cork a fully qualified driver. A year later we managed to buy a second-hand car. It was a Ford Popular, number HZ 6789. It made many journeys south.

# The Youth Club

Seventy years ago when we were school children, there was little talk of youth clubs but forty years later when our children were approaching their teenage years their constant pleading persuaded us to allow them join the newly formed youth club in Beragh. Soon after they joined, there were regular requests from those in charge of the club, for adults to help supervise on nights when the youngsters met and, more urgently, to help at committee levels. I volunteered to join the committee as they met less often and was likely to be less noisy.

I had simply no experience of youth clubs or indeed committee meetings, and rather than increase the numbers, I played little part. But less than two years later, the numbers attending the committee meetings had fallen and myself and three or four others were left in charge. When Beragh Youth Club was first formed, all functions and meetings were held in the parish hall. This meant that each piece of equipment had to be taken from and returned to the adjoining store before and after every session. In 1975 the new primary school in Beragh was opened and the old school had become vacant. It was available for youth club purposes but required a substantial amount of repairs and modifications. Even in those bygone days, renovations and extensions to a building cost a lot of money and our club's funds were low, practically non-existent.

Probably more experienced committee members would have ignored the situation, but the promise of some voluntary help and the availability of a grant, persuaded us to take on the mammoth task. Even the paper work and correspondence meant months of toil before we were allowed to commence with the repairs. Later we were to learn that the returns from many well supported fund-raising events, together with a generous grant, failed to keep pace with the expenditure and before the job was completed we found ourselves in debt to the extent of thousands of pounds.

Then, when all seemed lost, we had a stroke of luck. One day we were having a chat with a Priest who also had a problem, but of a different nature. It transpired he had some interest in a brood mare. This mare was the mother of a well-bred two-year-old filly. It was a fine looking animal but unfortunately it did not grow to the required height to be a best seller. It was suggested we would offer her as the prize in a draw for Beragh Youth Club. At first the suggestion was laughed at but a week later it was again discussed and we got the go-ahead.

Two thousand books of tickets, each bearing the photo and pedigree of the filly were printed and posted to all parts of the country. Special attention was given to Bookmakers Offices and to Pubs. The returns from that draw were unbelievable. Not only were most of the tickets sold, but also in a few cases, more books were requested. When the expenses of rearing the filly were paid, and all the building debt cleared, we had a few pounds left, which enabled us to buy an old school bus. For the next couple of years the bus was used to convey children to and from the club and to visit other clubs. We also made trips to museums in Dublin and Belfast and to catch the boat at Belfast on our way to the Isle of Man.

While the bus was used mostly on routine journeys, it did make two very memorable trips. One was a weeklong camping holiday in the South of Ireland. It was in 1985 and although that year is on record as being one of the wettest summers in a lifetime, we got five days and nights without rain. When we started off, the back of the bus was packed full of camping equipment, sleeping bags, gas stoves, kettles and tea pots, and a couple of frying pans. Every person was responsible for his or her own plates, cups and cutlery. We had a good supply of home baked bread, several boxes of cereal, and enough bacon and sausages to last a day or two. We had two or three dozen free range eggs and some milk. We could always top up as we travelled along.

We were fifteen in number and space was limited on the bus because of the camping equipment, but no one seemed to mind. We started off on a Monday morning and headed off to the Cooley Mountain in Co. Louth. Arrangements had been made with the committee of a parish which was allowing us to use their hall on the first night of our expedition. After we had our meal a small number of local youths joined us and there was dancing and gigging for a short while before we settled down.

Next morning we were afoot quite early, and as the cooking facilities in the kitchen were available, it was not long until the smell of fried rashers filled the hall. We ate a hearty breakfast before starting off on the second stage of our journey. The plan was to spend most of the day climbing Cooley Mountain. Then we would have a cup of tea, and in the evening, make our way to the village of Collon where we were told we would find the old gate lodge at the end of the village and we were welcome to stay there for the night.

All went according to plan until we arrived at the gate lodge. Then, just as soon as the bus had come to a halt, three or four girls jumped out and ran into the lodge. A second bunch followed at a slower pace but as they reached the door, the first lassies came running out screeching, "mice, mice, it's crawling with mice!" When we inspected the building we did indeed find evidence of mice. Now with all due respect for those who offered us shelter, I may have stopped the bus at the wrong gatehouse. We never did find out. What I do know is, you seldom win an argument with fourteen teenagers. They wanted to camp out, so, we boarded the bus and went in search of a camping site.

By some stroke of luck we found ourselves at Mellifont Abbey, home of the Cistercians Order. When we explained our position, we were told to drive round the back and we would find ample space. We did as we were told and found a large park in which there were a few trees.Near to one of these trees, and about one hundred yards away from the spot where we stopped, we could see a well constructed tent around which a number of uniformed youths were moving. Nearby the blaze from a big log fire leaped high into the air.

While the boys of our group attempted to erect the tents, the girls toiled at the gas stoves in an effort to boil water and fry bacon and sausages. We had scarcely started when two of the boys from the other camp approached us and enquired if we intended to camp there for the night. I told them that we did and that we had asked and were given permission. I asked was there a problem. He explained that the rules for their group stated that they must not camp in a park where there were other groups camping. I explained that we were only a small youth club who knew nothing about such rules, but if we were breaking someone's rules, we would move on when we had our meal. He seemed delighted with this news and explained. "If you are only a youth club, and are not putting up a flag, it did not break the rules." In fact they offered to help with the tents and to light our fire. It was a cold night and late when the meal was finished. The Scout's fire was still alight as one by one our group crawled into their sleeping bags and soon all was quiet. I slept in the bus.

Our plans for the next day were to visit Glenda Lough. We had an early start and a hurried breakfast as we had a deadline to meet. Fr. Mc.Parland, our parish curate, was to join us at Slane and accompany us for the next couple of days. When we arrived at the arranged meeting spot on the banks of the Boyne a pleasant surprise awaited us. The Priest had arrived, and, in a second car were two members of our youth club with a large joint of roast meat and all the trimmings. Not only was there enough to quell our hunger but sufficient leftovers to provide us with another good meal later in the evening.

When we had partaken, our "dinner service" got a speedy wash up and we were soon on the road again. It was a glorious evening when we arrived at the serene environment of Glenda Lough and St.Kevin's monastic settlement. Then, in the evening as the shadows lengthened we drove along close by the Avonmore River in the Vale of Avondale searching for a suitable picnic spot for our evening meal and to pitch camp for the night. Three times we stopped and each time the midges drove us back into the bus. We had little choice but to drive to higher ground where there was a slight breeze. Along a little narrow road we stopped at an old-time farmhouse. A man advanced in years, with weather-beaten face and unruly hair answered our knock at the door. When we told him of our predicament, he turned towards an oldish woman who appeared beside him. They seemed to come to the conclusion that we were harmless. He took a couple of steps from the door and pointed towards a field across the road. "Would yez be all right over there?" says he.

The field he pointed to was bare of grass and had several bunches of whins, but it was fine and dry and easily accessible for the bus. Better still, there was no protests from my passengers.

As we moved towards the bus again the old lady called out "Is there anything else yez might be wanting?" I said we were in need of some fresh water. "There's a pump in the yard" was the reply. We thanked her and drove into the field where we found plenty of space for the tents in the shelter of the whins. As the young people disembarked I could hear muffled voices and feared something was amiss. When I stepped out I saw the trouble. This time there was no evidence of mice but there sure was evidence of sheep. I watched for a moment or two and said nothing. Then a couple of lads ran to the hedge and broke branches off a tree. With these they started sweeping and others quickly joined them. It became like a game and soon the space was spotless. A ground sheet was spread and the kettles boiled. In a very short time we devoured the leftovers of the previous meal and afterwards there were games of tig, hide-and-seek and blind-mans-buff amongst the whins. That night it was almost dark before the tents were erected.

Next morning it was back to cornflakes, sausages and eggs before we started up-hill towards Sally Gap before turning west, aiming for Co. Galway. We had a couple of breaks for refreshments and night found us somewhere in the midlands. My idea was to give towns or villages a wide berth in the late evenings as the sound of music, especially disco music, could give rise to a number of requests and no doubt, problems.

As we journeyed along, a pleasant looking man was closing the gate that led into a big field where hay had been saved and most of the bales had been removed. I stopped the bus and asked if he knew of any place where we could camp for the night. He looked back into the field he was leaving and after a short pause he swung the gate open and said, "There's little harm yez can do in there." We thanked him as he waited to close the gate when we passed through. It was a very big flat field, probably more than ten acres in size, and we drove to the furthest corner where there was still a few dampish bales remaining. We had shelter behind the big thorn hedge and while the cooking was being done, the boys put up the tents and arranged the bales of hay as goal posts. After we had eaten, a game of football provided entertainment until one by one the players grew weary and decided to lay their heads on the makeshift pillows beneath the canvas.

Next day was uneventful. We travelled slowly and made short stops in a few small towns. Night found us camping in the shelter of a stone wall in North Galway. No one seemed to be hungry as we had nibbled and eaten many times during the day. A cup of tea satisfied most before we retired.

Saturday morning was still fine and our aim was to camp in Donegal on the last night of our trip. The weather was fine until after midday, but as we continued on our journey, raindrops appeared on the windscreen and as the shower got heavier camping took on a whole new meaning. When mealtime came we chose to opt for take-away instead of cooking and as the hours passed the rain continued. Pitching camp had now lost its appeal.

It was after eight o'clock when I suggested that it might be best if we changed our course and started for home. Thankfully there were no refusals, in fact I think they were pleased, but none more so than myself. When we reached Glenties, as the motoring addicts would say, it was 'right hand down and keep going'. Mobile phones were not to be had back then but we used the first call box we saw to let our folk know that we were on our way home.

While all of the young people who travelled still say they thoroughly enjoyed the trip I too can say I have no regrets, but, neither do I have trouble in relating to the lines of the poem:

"Safe is the roof, and soft the bed, the sailor finds ashore."

I can testify the camper finds at home!

The second road trip was also a memorable one. As we grow older it is not easy to remember what one was doing at a specific time on a specific day twenty-eight years earlier. But I suppose there are a few incidents in our lives that leave a mark on our memory, which do not erode with the passing of time.

The 29th and 30th of September 1979 are two such days for a majority of the population of Ireland. As one of those millions of people, I can clearly recall the visit of Pope John Paul 11 to Ireland, and our preparation and journey to Ballybrit racecourse, and to be amongst the 250,000 young people from every corner of the Isle who assembled to welcome him.

Just after mid-day on Saturday 29th two buses, carrying over seventy excited young people, left Beragh on the first stage of the journey. A large Ulster Bus had a qualified driver and I was instructed, as driver of the second small bus, to keep close and not allow the group to be separated in the latter stages of the journey. We were to drive to Tuam and rest at the Club Amarillo for a few hours before completing the journey. We arrived at the club short-ly after six o'clock and partook of our packed lunch. We had been instructed that we were to share a large hall with another group of similar numbers and that lights would go out at ten o'clock. Nothing on earth would have prepared one for the commotion and noise of the next couple of hours. Knapsacks, hold-alls, rugs and sleeping bags littered the floor. In a corner, one of our club leaders strummed the guitar. He was accompanied by a couple of musicians from the other group, but the volume of the ballad singers, who were in full voice, drowned their music. For quite a while those who dared to get into their sleeping bags were in dan-ger of being trampled under-foot by the milling crowd.

On the stroke of ten there was a tremendous cheer as the lights flashed and dropped down to a dim nightlight. Then, as gradually as night follows day, the volume of noise dropped to a soft mur-mur and all was still. Earlier in the night I had squatted in a small recess at the side of the stage and after listening to the quiet for some time, I managed to fall asleep.

I have no idea of how long I was asleep, but when I stirred and had the uncomfortable feeling that someone or something was moving close to me. As I opened my eyes I could see a very large, well-polished boot little more than a foot away from my nose. As I moved my head I discovered there was two of them and in them stood a great big Garda Sergeant. He explained that he was about to put on the light. It was 2.30 a.m. and time to be on the move again. We had just one hour to get a bite to eat, refill our flasks with boiling water, and get our luggage back onto the bus by 3.30

for the sixteen-mile journey to Ballybrit Racecourse.

For the first few miles we seemed to be alone in the darkness but soon all became alive as houses were lit up and cars and buses of all shapes and sizes slowly made their way to the different parks. It was 4.30.am when we were ushered into the grandstand area but the seats were already full and we sat on the steps. At seven o'clock we were asked to stand, as there were still four thousand more young people waiting to get in. By dawn, as far as the eye could see in any direction there was a mass of faces. It was ten o'clock when a little yellow dot appeared in the sky and as the helicopter approached, the waving and the roar of the crowd surely let Pope John Paul 11 know that the young people of Ireland welcomed him.

Today, most of those same young people are adults in our society. I wonder do they remember his words:

*"Young people of Ireland I love you,*
*Today the pope belongs to the youth of Ireland.*
*Tomorrow Ireland will depend on you.*
**I believe in each one of you."**

In the early days of 1985 hopes were raised by talk of a cease-fire in the troubles in Northern Ireland and the following lines were written:

## A dream come true

*The twelfth day of Christmas,*
*A New Year, six days old;*
*The flickering flame of Peace that burns*
*How can we make it hold.*
*Not only hold but spread, engulf*
*All of the human race,*
*Then put an end to war and strife*
*And suffering and disgrace.*

*We're promised pounds, a thousand fold;*
*But money peace won't buy,*
*We've got to curb our selfish ways*
*And thoughts of hate deny;*
*We must build bonds of hope and love,*
*And choose words soft and caring,*
*Be worthy of each others trust,*
*By patience and by sharing.*

*Let's not depend on rules or laws*
*Based on wealth or power,*
*But pray for wisdom and insight*
*To light our darkest hour.*
*And let who's humble, humbler be*
*Not boast of greater learning;*
*But pray that God will grant the peace*
*For which this World is yearning.*

# Cork

Mary and I made many trips down south. Whilst many of the journeys were for short stay visits, occasionally we found time to explore and gain local knowledge of places of interest.

Amongst many of the places we explored were:

*Assolas House, Kanturk*

Assolas is a charming 17th century house, set among ancient trees, with lawns sweeping down to the river. In 1714 Reverend Francis Gore took up residence. Every night during his 34 years at Assolas, Reverend Gore hung a lantern high on the wall of the house, shining its light on the waters of the ford to guide the travellers on their way. It is reported that, during this period, highwaymen often lurked at dangerous crossings for innocent victims. Assolas House was always open to receive the wounded should they fall prey to roaming bands. This warm friendly light became so well known that the house by the ford took its name in Gaelic, the spoken language of the time, as 'Atha Solas' the ford of the light, later adapted to its English version, Assolas.

# Edel Quinn's house, Kanturk.

Edel Mary Quinn (1907–1944) was an Irish lay missionary.
Born in Kanturk, County Cork, Edel Quinn felt a call to religious
life at a young age, but ill health prevented it. She joined the
Legion of Mary in Dublin at age 20 and gave herself completely to
its work in the form of helping the poor in the slums of Dublin.
In 1936, at age 29 and dying of tuberculosis, Edel became a Legion
of Mary Envoy, a missionary to East and Central Africa. Fighting
her illness, in seven and a half years she established hundreds of
Legion branches and councils in today's Tanzania, Kenya, Uganda,
Malawi, and Mauritius. She died in Nairobi, Kenya, of tuberculosis and is buried there in the Missionaries' Cemetery.

# Gougane Barra.

Gougane Barra is a settlement, west of Macroom in County Cork, Ireland. The name Gougane Barra derives from the Irish: "Guagán Barra", meaning Barra's retreat enclosed by mountains. According to tradition, St. Finbar built his monastery on the island here in the 6th century. Along with being a place of pilgrimage it is also considered to be one of the top beauty spots in Ireland. Nestling in the Sheehy mountains, Gougane Barra is the source of the River Lee. The tiny chapel on the island is recognised as the smallest in Ireland. The beauty of this spot, surrounded by heather clad mountains and forests, is enough to take one's breath away.

### Gougane Barra
*by J. J. Callanan*

*There is a green island in lone Gougane Barra,*
*Where Allua of songs rushes forth as an arrow;*
*In deep-valley'd Desmond - a thousand wild fountains*
*Come down to that lake from their homes in the mountains.*
*There grows the wild ash, and a time stricken willow*
*Looks chidingly down on the mirth of the billow;*
*As, like some gay child, that sad monitor scorning,*
*It lightly laughs back to the laugh of the morning.*

# The Battle of Knocknanuss

In 1625 Charles I became king of England and immediately set about restoring Catholicism as the official religion. The English parliament led by the puritan Oliver Cromwell with his followers opposed this, which brought about the English civil war. The local Battle of Knocknanuss in 1647 was the single largest battle in this conflict. Approximately 3,500 men were killed. The hill itself is now the property of Billy Coleman who was Irelands most successful rally driver ever.

# Franciscan Friary Buttevant.

This abbey was founded in 1254 by Donal de Barry, grandson of Philip de Barry, and dedicated to Thomas a Beckett. The ruined abbey, of which only the church still remains, contains a skeleton-filled two storey crypt together with some well preserved sarcophagi's. It is understood that the bones of those who died in the Battle of Knocknanaus were laid to rest in the crypt here. It is locally referred to as the 'house of bones'.

# Buttevant

The steeplechase originated in Ireland in the 18th century. The first steeplechase is said to have been the result of a wager in 1752 between Mr. Cornelius O'Callaghan and Mr. Edmund Blake, racing four miles (6 km) cross-country from Buttevant Church to St. Leger Church in Doneraile, in Cork, Ireland. The horses raced from church steeple to church steeple, hence the term 'steeplechase'. This sign commemorating the event is adjacent to the Franciscan Friary on the gable of Moloney's bar.

# Kanturk Castle

This is one of the largest and finest castles ever undertaken by a Gaelic Chieftain and was built for Dermot MacDonagh McCarthy, Lord of Duhallow. Much local legend surrounds the castle and the reasons why the roofing was never completed despite the rows of heavy corbelling prepared for the parapets. It is said when work was abandoned, the coloured window glass was dumped in a nearby stream, known as 'The Blue Pool'. Local legend has it that the workmen were driven to exhaustion and that the blood of those who perished on the site was used to mix the mortar.

# Ballygiblin, 'The Great House'

Ballygiblin, the home of the Wrixon-Beecher family is known locally as 'The Great House'. In 1839 when the first Grand National was run, Captain Beecher was leading the race. He fell off his horse into a brook. The fence where he fell is now the most famous fence on the Aintree Racecourse known today as 'Beecher's Brook' On being dragged from the stream the disgruntled Captain was heard to mutter "Never did I think that water without whiskey could be so foul tasting!"

Sean Clifford was a local Cork storyteller who was welcome at every céilí house in the locality. The following two poems are from his vast repertoire:

GUIDE TO CORK

TRAVEL CATHERWOOD

*See Ireland & Scotland*

BY MOTOR COACH.

SEASON 1930.

Delightful Tours have been arranged, extending from One to Eleven Days.

Visiting Dublin, Vale of Avoca, Waterford, Cork, Glengarriff, Killarney, Connemara, the Highlands of Donegal, and Portrush.

Glasgow, Melrose, Edinburgh, Trossachs, Aberdeen and the Highlands.

Fares, including First Class Travel, Hotel Accommodation, and all gratuities:—

| IRISH TOURS, | 4 Days | £7 | 7 | 0 | |
| " | " | 7 | 13 | 5 | 0 { From |
| " | " | 11 | 18 | 10 | 0 } Belfast |
| " | " | 9 | 16 | 0 | 0 From |
| " | " | 11 | 18 | 10 | 0 Cor. |
| SCOTTISH TOURS | 7 | 13 | 15 | 0 ,, Belfast |
| " | " | 7 | 12 | 10 | 0 ,, Glasgow |

Competent Guide-Lecturer accompanies each tour

H. M. S. CATHERWOOD, LIMITED,

UPPER LIBRARY ST., BELFAST, EDEN QUAY, DUBLIN.

Illustrated Brochure and Full Particulars from our Agent—

Mr. G. HEFFERNAN, 21, South Mall, Cork.

For Classified Index to Advertisers see page 11

80

GUIDE TO CORK

'Phone 683.

KINCORA CAFE

COOK STREET, CORK

Under Personal Supervision of Mrs. P. T. O'CONNOR.

EXCELLENT CUISINE : :

: : QUICK SERVICE

Table d'Hote Luncheons and Dinners Open to Non-Residents.

WEDDING BREAKFASTS ——A SPECIALITY——

Restaurant Open all day Sunday and Wednesday. One minute from G.P.O.

TARIFF :

| Bed and Breakfast - | - | 5/6 |
| Luncheon (3 Course) | - | 2/- |
| 1 to 3.30 p.m. | | |
| Afternoon Teas | - | - | 1/- |

Residential Terms on application.

For Classified Index to Advertisers see page 11

83

## *School Bus*
### *by Sean Clifford*

*I was passing the schoolhouse one morning,*
*The bus, it had stopped at the gate.*
*With cars and the bus the road it was jammed,*
*So I just had to sit there and wait.*
*Somehow I pitied the children.*
*As they climbed from the cars and the bus,*
*Though they hadn't to foot it along to the school,*
*They would never have memories like us.*

They would never have memories of wading to school,
When the snow was knee deep on the ground,
Or having a slide or a hunker
On every ice patch that they found.
Somehow we never paid heed to the cold,
And we hadn't a cough or a sneeze,
But now, by Jove, the school would be closed
If the heat drops to fifteen degrees.

We were snow-balling one winter's day
When old Rodger ran out from his shop
I'll be calling the Guards in a moment, he yelled
If this bloody racket don't stop.
Sure I know all your names and I'll tell them
If you don't get to hell out of here,
Flash Murphy had a snowball as big as his head
And he hit him, spot on, in the ear.

Then poor Miss O'Reilly God bless her,
I hope she's in Heaven today,
But I tell you, we'll never get there,
If yon old doll gets her way
She said we were the result of bad rearing
A bold and troublesome crew,
Of all the tinkers that passed by her gate
We were the worst that she knew.

She had a nice flock of White Leghorn Chickens,
With a great big Rhode Island cock,
She said he was pure bred and registered,
And came from good pedigree stock.
The way that he strutted about the yard,
You would think he was lazy as sin,
But he could sprint like a greyhound,
When a chase for a hen would begin.

194

*He was out in the yard one evening,*
*With his head in the air, and him crowing.*
*Smiley took aim through the bars of the gate,*
*And gave him a whack of a stone.*
*When we were passing next morning,*
*She was mixing pigs' feed in a tub*
*She ran to the gate, her eyes blazing,*
*Like a tiger after losing its cub*

*Well the names that she called us that morning,*
*I never heard since or before*
*But I can assure you it wasn't*
*A chuisle, alana, a stór.*
*There was a cow clap where Smiley was standing,*
*And although it was a bit thin,*
*He managed to get a lump on his foot,*
*And he landed it right on her chin!*
*Smiley didn't wait to hear what she said,*
*He took off like a scalded cat,*
*He wasn't at school when I got the length,*
*Nor he never came back after that.*

*I have great memories of finding birds nests*
*As we searched all the bushes and trees*
*And manys a thorn we got in our feet,*
*And scrapes on our legs and our knees.*
*Smiley Cavanagh and myself found a goldfinch's nest,*
*Well concealed in a big hawthorn tree,*
*We were afraid Pat Reilly might find it,*
*We just wondered how long it might be.*

*He was waiting beside it one morning*
*So we knew that the nest had been found,*
*He waited till we were beside him*
*Then he tossed it right out on the ground.*

We pulled down his pants when we caught him,
Then put him face down on the grass
Smiley grabbed a big bunch of nettles
And slapped them right down on his a--.

Well he cursed and he swore like a trooper,
And I never heard such a yell,
When Smiley said, turn right him over,
Sure I must do the front side as well.
The teacher must have heard what had happened,
For next week when Pat failed in his tests,
He said, you are bad at your lessons
And also at robbing birds nests.

'Tis well I remember the summer,
I remember the first golden rule.
We polished our shoes, put them up on the loft,
And we went on the bare-ones to school.
We loved to splash in the puddles
After rain on a warm summer day,
We walked in the bog and the heather
There were so many games we could play.

Sometimes we did get a bad bruise
When we trod on a rough bit of stone
And a nail or sharp bit of wire.
Could stab you right in to the bone.
But we never were sent to the doctor,
There was no injections or pills,
Our mother was both nurse and doctor,
And she knew the cure for all ills.

Bread poultice was placed on an abscess
Linseed poultice drew out the pus.
Castor oil was administered sometimes,

*It kept us on the move without fuss.*
*Nettle tay helped bring out the measles,*
*Hot whey was the cure for a cold.*
*And a sharp rod that was kept near the fire,*
*Cured those who were naughty or bold.*

*Now these are a few of the memories,*
*I recalled as I sat at the gate,*
*There is still a lot more I remember,*
*But I have not got time to relate.*
*I know that the kids looked quite happy,*
*As they climbed from the cars and the bus,*
*But I think they'd be better of walking,*
*So that they could have memories like us.*

GUIDE TO CORK

CORK

Hotel
Metropole

The Finest Unlicensed Hotel in Ireland
Electric Elevator and all modern Conveniences
Hot & Cold Water and every Modern Requirement

16/- PER DAY          BED AND     8/9
(Inclusive)          BREAKFAST

FREE GARAGE FOR 20 CARS.
Phone 100 (3 lines).          Night Porter.

CORK

For Classified Index to Advertisers see page 11

GUIDE TO CORK

HOSKING'S

Hotel and

Restaurant
Prince's Street,
CORK

3 Course Luncheon   2/-
Choice of Three Joints)
Bed & Breakfast from 5/-
Daily Terms      -      10/-

:  Hot and Cold Water  :
Electric Light throughout

Telephone 1417 Cork.

For Classified Index to Advertisers see page 11
82

## O'Briens
*by Sean Clifford*

*O'Brien's Sometimes when I'm dreaming it's so clearly I recall*
*The nights when we went dancing, in O'Brien's Super Hall,*
*I still can see them queuing, those happy laughing pairs*
*And watch them as they climb the steps, to the new dance floor upstairs.*
*Admission was a half-a-crown, dancing ten till three*
*We would hang about till after twelve, and get in for half the fee.*
*The hall went on for years and years, aye, twenty years or more,*
*'Twas famous for its music and its inlaid maple floor.*

*The mineral bar was down the steps, as was the cloakroom too,*
*And quite adjacent to them there was a spacious loo.*
*The local clubs each had a night to hold their annual dance,*
*It was their way of raising funds and boosting their finance*
*Fine Gael and Labour too, and of course Fianna Fáil*
*They held their dances every year, and the Huntsmen held a ball.*
*O'Briens was the venue for each annual event*
*But it closed its doors so tightly, for the forty days of Lent.*

*It was the grandest dance hall, the finest in the land,*
*But what use would a dance hall be if you didn't have a band.*
*Musicians came from near and far in the bygone age,*
*As talented musicians as ever graced a stage.*
*From Tralee came Jimmy Rohan, the Arcadians too from there,*
*And Kevin Flynn, a seven piece, I think he came from Cahir.*
*Paddy Benson and Des Fretwell played all their tunes with pride,*
*And then came John Mc Mahon who hailed from Shannon side.*

*Cork city sent Pat Crowley and Dolly Butler too,*
*The Regent and the Regal, to name but just a few.*
*Michael "O" from Buttevant, Donie Regan came as well,*
*I bet you all remember that famous man Mick Dell.*
*Now I know you're thinking that somehow I forgot*

*All those powerful céilí bands that played upon this spot.*
*The Gallowglass, the Assoroe, the Blarney, Donald Ring,*
*The Fitzgerald man from Donegal, he was the Céilí King.*

*Galway sent five sisters, who played and sang so true*
*Their brother Sean was on the drums, their name, O'Donoghue.*
*Malachy Sweeney was the next, from a border town he came,*
*And then a man called Pickering of northern céilí fame.*
*Then we had some local ones, who were just as grand,*
*Like Mike and Dan O'Mahony and the Shandrum Céilí Band,*
*And our neighbour Paddy Barrett, sure we never will forget,*
*His music taught us how to waltz and dance the polka set.*

*Another one I near forgot, now that would have been a sin*
*For none could match Roy Campbell, When the Saints Come Marching In.*
*There was always special nights when big stars hit the town*
*O'Brien's was completely packed, for such persons of renown.*
*I remember one occasion, the year was fifty eight.*
*When Bridie Gallagher came to town, the attraction it was great.*
*They closed the doors at ten o'clock, I was nearly late,*
*I boldly elbowed through the crowd, it was like a Fleadh,*
*I could hear Bridie singing, The Boys From The Co. Armagh.*

*A few months passed, and the next big do, O'Brien's was to see*
*Was the carnival dance on a Sunday night, it was on from nine till three.*
*I got there about twelve o'clock and commotion reigned supreme,*
*All because a crack appeared in the main supporting beam.*
*Fr. Mc. was at the door, he was looking quite forlorn,*
*If someone doesn't do something quick, the whole parish it will mourn.*
*But Paddy Greaney (rest his soul) arrived with saw and hammer,*
*And managed to put in a prop in spite of all the clamour.*
*The band played on, the dancers danced, we danced the whole night long,*
*And thanks to poor auld Paddy we heard the Soldier's Song.*

*Now I know I've jogged your memories and I know what wise men say,*
*Memories are precious things that no one can take away.*
*If you are in Newmarket and walking up the street*
*You may think you hear the sweet music and the sound of dancing*
*feet,*
*Take no notice, carry on, for like me you'll surely know,*
*It's the echoes of the dancing nights in O'Brien's long ago.*

The following poem is based on a true story. A young boy helped his father who was a worker on a large estate. The lad was badly treated by the heir to the estate. He studied hard at school, went to college and became a doctor. Later in life as he worked in a local hospital he treated his former master who was very ill and close to death. When I heard the tale being told in the West of Ireland, I thought it would sound better if told in rhyme. People and place names are fictitious.

## The Estate

*The estate looked vast and fertile, beneath the mountain tall,*
*Its boundaries marked distinctly, by a sturdy limestone wall.*
*The squire travelled widely, oft with dog and gun,*
*He wed a titled lady and they had an heir, a son.*

*The domain had many workers, one was Jack Mc Dade,*
*He was an honest servant, a carpenter by trade.*
*He wooed and wed a handsome lass, she too worked for the squire,*
*Her job was in the manor house, her name was Ann McGuire.*

*Jack and Ann lived happily, life was full of joy,*
*And almost two years latter, God blessed them with a boy.*
*Ann strove hard to keep her job, and tend to little John,*
*Jack too worked on till late at night, he would start again at dawn.*

*Years seemed to pass so quickly, young John grew strong and able.*
*When he was only ten years old, he was working in the stable.*
*He was unfairly treated, by the heir of the estate,*
*Given most unpleasant tasks, and often kept on late.*

*Then Ann's health started failing, her face grew thin and pale,*
*Soon she was bedridden, her body weak and frail.*
*John and Jack did nurse her well, they did their very best,*
*But John was still a schoolboy when they laid poor Ann to rest.*

*In the sorrowful months that followed, John searched so hard to find,*
*Some ray of hope or sparkle, when a new thought crossed his mind.*
*He discussed it with his father, and was pleased to hear him say,*
*"John, when you become a doctor, it will be my brightest day."*

*Well John did become a doctor, after years of toil and strife,*
*Though he often worked in foreign lands, he wed an Irish wife*
*And almost twelve years later, he saw his father's smiling face,*
*When he returned to Ireland, to take a top consultant's place.*

*While doing his rounds one morning, John paused beside a bed,*
*He gazed long at the patient, then the chart he read.*
*The patient's wan and feeble hand beckoned him bend low,*
*And in barely audible trembling words, he told his tale of woe.*

*"My father owned the Manor House, beside the Devil's Bit,*
*You helped down at the stables a willing lad and fit.*
*I did not play my part back then, to help on the estate,*
*I ask you to forgive me now, I hope it's not too late."*

*"My parents died ten years ago, their boat sank out at sea,*
*They were buried near the Devil's Bit, The estate was willed to me.*
*Sadly I was careless, and didn't manage well,*
*The debts became un-payable, and I was forced to sell."*

"Still the urge to live a carefree life, to me, was very strong,
What cash remained when debts were paid, it did not last me long.
Soon friends and pals deserted me; I was left alone,
No wife or child to comfort me, no place to call my own."

"I've slept at railway stations, sometimes beneath the sky,
No pillow for my weary head, no roof to keep me dry.
For months I've had this aching pain, drink kept it at bay,
I was taken here when I collapsed, three weeks ago today."

"Alas, for me the course is run, my days on earth are few,
But there's still one special favour I humbly ask of you.
In a Churchyard near the Devil's Bit, my parent's bones do lie,
Please place my corpse beside them, for it's soon that I must die."

"I have no relations; my friends have proved untrue,
This solitary family heirloom, I now bequeath to you.
Then from beneath his pillow, he took a watch off purest gold.
My one and last possession, it is now yours to hold."

"Twas presented to my Great Granddad, the old estates first Squire,
For rescuing the children, from a raging school-house fire,"
No further words were spoken, but John lingered for a while,
Until the body stopped it's breathing, and the lips bore a little smile.

# The Forth Chapel

After their marriage in 1991 our daughter Avril and Michael Monaghan made their home in the townland of Aughadarragh, close to the primary school and about two miles from the Forth Chapel. The Forth Chapel stands on a site quite close to the spot where Mass was said away back in the penal days. It is on record that the west gable was blown down in the night of the big wind in 1839. The stained glass window to the left of the main Altar in the Church was dedicated to the memory of Archbishop John Joseph Hughes D. D.

Archbishop Hughes was born in 1797 in the townland of Anboughan, about one mile from the forth chapel and in his young days he worked with his father in the grounds of Favor Royal as a gardener. In 1816 his father and brother emigrated to

America. It was some time later before John was able to join them and the family was re-united. As the family prospered John was able to realise his ambition and attend the seminar. He was ordained in 1826. He became Co-adjutor bishop in 1838. In 1850 he was appointed Archbishop. Eight years later he was to lay the foundation stone of St. Patrick's cathedral in New York.

In more recent years the cottage in Annaboughan where Archbishop Hughes was born was taken down stone by stone. Each stone was carefully numbered. They were taken to the Folk Park at Omagh and rebuilt in exactly the same style as the original cottage

Standing at the door of the Forth Chapel and looking westward over Lumfords Glen, one has a magnificent view of Knockmany Forest and the site of the Cairn, Ania's cove or Grave.

When we speak of Knockmany Forest the name of another famous person comes to mind. It is that of Rose Kavanagh the renowned poetess who was born in the townland of Killadroy in 1859. Her mother was a cousin of Archbishop Hughes. Rose spent the first ten or twelve years of her short life in Killadroy and attended primary school in Seskinore. In her early teenage years the family moved to Knockmany in the parish of Augher. There they lived close to the river Blackwater. We are told that Rose was a pupil at the Convent School in Omagh for some time. It is likely that she was a boarder there as daily travel to and from Augher would have been difficult in those bygone days.

When next we hear of Rose she has moved to Dublin. Although her qualifications and her early work in the city may have been Art related, it was her ability to write that came to the notice of Charles K. Kickam, the then editor of, 'The Monthly Press'. It was he who after reading some of her poems referred to her as, 'The Rose of Knockmany. She was also to receive praise and encouragement from W.B.Yeats. The words of the lovely poem referring to her birthplace is amongst the best of the many beautiful verses she penned.


## *A Reminiscence*
*By Rose Kavanagh 1859–1891*


*Oh, Killadroy, thy name revered, I see you in my dreams,*
*When often in my school days, I wandered by your streams,*
*The farmers' white-washed houses that adorn your hills and braes,*
*Recall old memories of the past and of my youthful days.*

*It's eight and twenty years ago since last thy hill I trod,*
*No doubt some friends of those bright days now lie beneath the sod,*

It's true that I behold no more the fields where I did rove,
Around a place called Sleenge Bog and down to Greenmount Grove.

In spirit now I'll wander to that stream beside the mill,
They called it then the "Routin' Burn" – it ran by Wilson's Hill,
The Routin' Burn with "Grandma's Bed", there grows the wild, white rose,
Where Kavanagh spent her childhood days, ere her name to fame arose.

From Greenmount West the road it wends to dear old Seskanore,
That village yet so dear to me may blessings on it pour.
The healthy western breezes there I know are blowing still,
Around the old plantation and the top of the Wood Hill.

Enclosed within the chapel yard there stood the National school,
Where McAleeer, our teacher, then, did wield the cane and rule.
Those boys and girls have grown now, for some life's battles o'er,
While others found an exile's home upon a distant shore

Oh, how I wish that I could stand upon my native hills and view,
The furze and hedge-rows shining all in the morning dew.
I hope ere long to spend my days where wild winds sigh and moan,
Adown the hills and valleys 'mid the trees in green Tyrone.

# The Touch of a Hand

Some time before our last wedding anniversary in 1998 I had written the lines of the poem that follows for my wife Mary. Later the words were put to music by the Hurson family, whose mother was a close neighbour and friend of Mary's. Mary heard the initial recording but, sadly, because of the tragedy, the work was never completed.

## The Touch of a Hand

*Down hearted I sat in the chapel,*
*My mind was not focused on prayer,*
*Then I saw a handsome young stranger,*
*Climb up the old wooden stair.*
*I vowed that somehow I would meet her,*
*And that night I was holding her hand,*
*As we danced to the sound of the music,*
*Played by St. Pats Céilí Band.*

*And when the last dance was over,*
*I asked could I see her again,*
*She said, "I am glad you have asked me,*
*But please give me time to explain.*
*My home is in sweet Knockavilling,*
*Away down in Cork by the Lee,*
*Sure you would not be home by the dawning,*
*If you were to come home with me."*

*"And tomorrow my ship it is sailing,*
*I'll be gone for a year and a day,*
*But I'll take you to sweet Knockavilling,*
*If you're faithful while I am away."*
*Each week she did write me a letter,*
*And I sent a note in return,*
*Our love it grew stronger and stronger,*
*Till our hearts like wildfire did burn.*

*It's strange how the load seems to lighten,*
*How blue skies can break through the grey,*
*How a smile from a charming young stranger,*
*Can banish life's troubles away.*
*And when love drifts by at that moment,*
*Then by the touch of a hand,*
*Two hearts can be bonded together,*
*And life is made glorious and grand.*

*When the long vigil was over,*
*And spring had returned once again,*
*The songbirds were welcoming Easter,*
*When Mary stepped down from the train.*
*We were wed in the long days of summer,*
*In a Chapel in Co. Tyrone,*
*Then we went down to sweet Knockavilling,*
*And kissed at the old Blarney Stone.*

*The years have now passed, four and forty,*
*And fate has been kind all the while,*
*Good times we have shared them together,*
*Dull moments made light by her smile.*
*Now all our fledglings have flown,*
*And sometimes when we're left alone,*
*We go down to sweet Knockavilling,*
*And call in at the old Blarney Stone.*

# August

The months of August and September were exceptionally busy times of the year in my young days. They were spoken of as the harvest time and any suggestion of going on holidays would not only have been frowned upon, it would have been forbidden. Harvest time was not a date you could have marked on a calendar. It was when the corn ripened and this varied from year to year. I've seen it turn a lovely golden colour and ripen in mid August but on a very late year it could remain green until early September.

Then, about 1960, farming methods changed considerably. On the advice of the Department of Agriculture most farmers gave up mixed farming and specialised in just one or two aspects. By offering grants for silage-making they encouraged farmers to give up tillage and haymaking. Harvest time, as we once knew it, is but a memory now to those of us who lived through and remember the hungry 1930s, and is history to those who were born after the 1939-1945 war. In later years the rush of work was over by mid-August and it was our favourite time for taking a break or a holiday.

But the 15th of August, which we regarded as a church holiday, had another great significance for our family. It was my wife's birthday. In the summer of 1998 we had discussed going on a pilgrimage but nothing definite was planned as both our daughters, Mary and Avril, had announced that they were expecting babies about that time. Although Mary lived in London and Avril lived at Aughadara, Augher, both girls kept in daily touch with their mother and with each other. Excitement was really heightened when it was announced that Avril was expecting twins.

As the dates of the confinements drew near shopping trips and phone messages became more frequent. Avril and her mother had arranged do some last minute shopping on the afternoon of the fifteenth of August, prior to my wife Mary flying to London on Monday the seventeenth to be with our daughter Mary (Brogan) when her baby was born.

At about one o'clock on Saturday we were just finished dinner when Avril (Monaghan) arrived in the yard. She had her twenty-month-old daughter Maura with her and they did not get out of the car. As my wife put on her coat, I enquired if she had money. She said she had a chequebook. I told her she might need some cash if they were having tea. She ran upstairs and then as she went out the door she said "We are away now, bye," and they were gone.

We at home were not definitely sure to which town they were going as they had not really decided when they had left. As was usual on a Church Holiday afternoon other members of the family went visiting or shopping but all would return in time to help with the milking and feeding.

Some time after they had gone I was in the chicken-house when I distinctly heard a bang or thud that I thought sounded like a bomb. I was surprised, as I understood the building I was in was almost sound proof. I had no idea what or where it was and I gave it little thought. My wife and myself had intended going out for a meal later in the evening as some member of the family had given us a voucher.

I was still out in the yard when the florist's van arrived with a bouquet of flowers for Mary's birthday. The driver told me he had heard that a bomb had exploded in Omagh but he did not hear of anyone being injured. A news bulletin shortly afterwards told a very different story and alarm bells were raised.

For a while we clung to the hope that they had gone to some other town but as time passed that hope faded. No words could describe the feeling of helplessness that set in as we watched and waited for the car to return.

Time meant nothing any more and news bulletins were now describing the scene of carnage. They also gave a list of telephone numbers that could be contacted. Understandably it was very difficult to get through and reception was often poor.

The answer was always the same. "Sorry, there is no one of that name on our list. Perhaps you would like to try the other numbers or ring back later." Another equally frustrating answer we heard so many times was, "Sorry, but we have your name and number and we will contact you if we have any news. Hours passed and no news came.

Three boys of the family went to Omagh in an effort to find any trace of them, but here again their way was blocked. They were compelled to go to the leisure centre where an incident room had been set up. It is not easy being obliged to stand aside and wait while strangers take over. It hurts to think that those you love most may be lying injured and in pain and wondering why you do not come to their assistance. It hurts even more when those who are missing are the ones who would spare no effort to rush to the aid of anyone in need.

By now any hope of Mary, Avril or little Maura coming home uninjured had faded completely and we had no choice but to contact members of the family who were working abroad or were on holiday.

Aidan, the youngest member of the family had gone to America and was working in New York. He was easily contacted and got an early flight home. Finbar had been in Germany for a good number of years. It was Monday before he got a flight. Patrick was on holiday in Wicklow. He had heard of the bomb in a news bulletin and had rung home. He came home right away. Fearghal came from Dublin and Niall was already home for the weekend from Galway. As I already stated our daughter Mary was in London. When she tried to book a flight she was informed that they could not allow her on a plane unless she got a line from her doctor stating that it was safe for her to fly. No doctor could be found to prescribe the necessary letter as her baby was due in a couple of day's time A number of Authorities and Councils, including Omagh were contacted but none came forward with a solution.

At nine o clock on Monday morning, Brian, Mary's husband, rang his place of work which was John Sisk & Sons, to inform them that he would be absent for a number of days. Upon understanding the difficulty the family were having in getting a flight to Ireland, the firm through their managing director, Mr. Pierce O'Shea, acted quickly. Very shortly afterwards the firm contacted Brian telling him to be at Denham Aer-drome (A small private aerodrome) at twelve o'clock and a plane would be waiting. The plane was small and had just three seats, one for the pilot and two for the passengers. Little Niamh, their eighteen-month-old daughter sat on Brian's knee. They flew at low altitude and although the flight was a little bumpy it was uneventful until they sighted St. Angelo Airport, Enniskillen. Here it seems communications had broken down and the airport was deserted. The pilot was unperturbed and assured his passengers that there was no problem. He circled the airport twice to get his bearings and then made a perfect landing.

But just as one problem was solved two more had arisen. First the plane needed to be refuelled and no one could be found to assist at this job and secondly the airport was surrounded by a high fence, the gates were locked and no one could be found to unlock them. Fortunately, Brian's brother had driven to the airport to collect them, and with the aid of his mobile phone, the gate-keeper was located. We understand that the pilot had to fly to the nearest airport to have the plane refuelled.

Meanwhile at home on Saturday evening a few relations and neighbours called but none could bring hopeful news. I think it was early on Sunday morning before a Belfast hospital rang and for a fleeting moment there was a brief glimmer of hope. They enquired if my wife had any particular body marks by which she could be identified. I told them that I knew of none and again the ray of hope was gone.

It is difficult to give precise times of different happenings but it was later on Sunday morning when Timothy and Declan, the boys who were at the leisure centre, were asked to go to the temporary morgue at the army camp to identify their sister Avril and little Maura.

Later, on Sunday evening, two fingerprint experts called at our house and spent hours searching for fingerprints to match those of Mary, my wife. After what seemed hours they made it known that they had found a perfect match on a flower vase.

The presence, comfort and help of relatives, friends and neighbours at that time were so much appreciated and will always be remembered. The happenings of the following days can best be described as a complete blur.

The remains of those who had died were released on Monday the seventeenth and each family was given a precise time to arrange for the removals. It was the afternoon when we gathered near the army camp to accompany the remains of Avril, her twin girls and little Maura to their home in Aughadara. Late in the same evening Mary's remains were taken to her home in Deroar.

To say that the happenings of the next couple of days were indescribable would be an understatement. The seemingly endless queues of people, the inability of myself or indeed all members of the family to match names and faces, or to make meaningful replies to the heartfelt words of sympathy offered, at a time when our lives had been cruelly torn apart, was not easy.

Amongst those who called at our house on Sunday evening was a lady who was one of the last to have been in touch with Mary, Avril, and little Maura. Her name was Sharon Robinson and she worked in S.D. Kell's shop. They had called into the shop and purchased some small items. As they were leaving Avril lifted Maura in her arms and the little girl waved and said 'bye-bye' to the staff in the shop. Everyone smiled as they went to the door. It was then the bomb exploded.

On Tuesday 18th of August Avril and her children were buried in a single grave after Requiem Mass in the ancient Forth Church near Augher.

On Wednesday 19th following the celebration Mass in the New Church in Beragh, Mary's remains were laid to rest in the grounds where the old Chapel stood, just a few yards from the spot where we were married on the 11th July 1956.

Forty-three years before, on that same spot, I first saw Mary as she walked up the stairs of the old church.

*Aiobheann on her communion day at her grandmother's graveside.*

*Aiobheann on her communion day at her mother's graveside.*
*Railed grave at the top right hand side of the photograph is that of the poet Rose Kavanagh.*

## The Fifteenth day of August

*The fifteenth day of August,*
*Nineteen ninety eight,*
*Tears still sting my tired eyes*
*As I recall that date*
*It was on that day of slaughter*
*Our daughter Avril lost her life*
*Along with her three children.*
*And Mary, my dear wife.*
*Many others were bereaved*
*As friends and neighbours died*
*Strangers too, when told the news*
*Just bowed their head and cried.*

*Three children from Buncrana died,*
*And two from far off Spain.*
*The little twins awaiting birth,*
*Were all amongst the slain.*
*Some few were just teenagers,*
*Whose lives were still a dream.*
*And others were beloved folk,*
*Good citizens, the cream.*
*Hundreds more were injured,*
*Some suffered dreadful pain.*
*In many homes that evening*
*Tears fell down like rain.*

*That morning we had promise,*
*Of happy days ahead*
*But ere the sun had sank in the west,*
*Thirty one lay dead.*
*Dozens more lay injured,*
*Hundreds cried with pain,*
*I ask, who planned this cruel act,*

*Or what did they hope to gain.*
*Most who died were shoppers,*
*Doing what most folks do,*
*Buying some essentials,*
*Or gifts for me or you,*

*We had thirty years of the troubles,*
*More than three thousand died.*
*Many homes were torn apart,*
*Too many tears were cried*
*Let's hope we've learned a lesson*
*And at any time again,*
*We'll not be tempted to go to war*
*Or to start inflicting pain.*
*In this old world there is enough,*
*And always some to spare*
*If every man would be content*
*When he has got his share,*
*If we could ask all those who died*
*I'll bet all would agree*
*If we choose to live in Peace*
*Then it's Love that holds the Key*

Massive crowds, many from the farthest flung counties of the island attended the funerals Two days after the funerals my daughter Mary (Brogan) went into the Erne Hospital at Enniskillen and her daughter Eilis was born that evening. On their departure from the hospital on the following day she and her husband Brian understood that it was necessary to register the birth of their child in Omagh before their return to London. But on the morning of their departure they found many obstacles in their path. Staff in the Omagh Registrars Office were of the opinion that the birth should have been registered at Enniskillen. The fact that they had booked their flights to London for that day seemed to make matters more difficult. It was even suggested that the mother and baby did not travel until further checks were made. It took more than an hour's pleading to get the matter resolved leaving little time to prepare for the departure.

In the immediate aftermath of the tragedy, and indeed to this present day, many kind people offer words of support and genuine sympathy. To each and every one of these people we are eternally grateful.

*Above: Joan Mary's sister, Mick Mary's husband, Bill Clinton and Timothy Mary's son.*

*Below: Avril's son Patrick being held by Aidan Monaghan. George Mitchell, Bill Clinton, Avril's daughter Aoibheann and her husband Mickey Monaghan.*

*Avril's family: Patrick, Mickey, Aoibheann and Eilisha.*

## Peace Please

*The year is young, the century new.*
*We've just seen out millennium two.*
*We've turned a page, all clean and white.*
*At last the future seemed so bright.*
*We'd thirty years of war, or more*
*Our eyes still wet our hearts still sore.*
*Those we loved, the best have died*
*Their babies buried by their side.*
*We prayed each day that killings would cease,*
*And begged the lord to send us peace.*
*Talks were held, elections run*
*Votes were counted, peace had won.*
*Politicians gathered on the day,*
*Their first demand a rise in pay.*
*Then an extended Christmas rest,*
*Arriving back to do their best*
*To make impossible demands,*

*No kindly smile or shake of hands.*
*The language used is such a shame,*
*Meant to hurt or cause great pain.*
*Yet in the country, far and wide,*
*Neighbours working side by side,*
*Laugh together enjoying life,*
*Without the slightest sign of strife.*
*And if by chance one falls in need,*
*Friend of every class and creed*
*Call to say how much they care*
*Offering gifts that they can spare.*
*At ploughing match or mart or fair*
*Farmers love to gather there.*
*Each with his usual tale of woe,*
*Debts and prices, hail and snow.*
*Oh how different life could be*
*If politicians care to see*
*The chance they have to make things good*
*If they'd act and speak like Christians should.*

## The end of the mile

We've read in the papers and heard on the news,
So many versions and wide-ranging views,
On effects of the troubles and long years of strife
Of pain and of suffering and great loss of life

Let's hope that it's over, we're at last on the way
To a happier future, a much brighter day
When we'll all live as Christians should
Working for peace and the communal good

Caring for those who have suffered and cried
With fondest remembrance for those who have died;
For although they have gone we know 'twas God's will
They are still very near and do love us still

So let's not dishonour or cause disrepute
By using their passing for a share in the loot;
It's time cruel words and quarrelling would cease
And allow all our loved ones to rest in peace.

For no-one can value the worth of a smile
Or the clasp of a hand on the long rugged mile
A word softly spoken when we're feeling the pace,
Or a tear gently brushed from a young grieving face.

The worth of these virtues just cannot be told
Nor the loss of a loved one be measured in gold
Though our hearts are still breaking, we must try to smile
They are waiting to greet us at the end of the mile.

*Church window in St. Joseph's Lismire, County Cork, dedicated to the memories of Mary Grimes, Avril Monaghan, Maura and the twins.*

# APPENDIX

1  **Brae**              A stretch of road with a steep gradient.

2  **Sheugh**            A drainage channel in a field or alongside a road.

3  **Céilí**             A friendly visit to a neighbour's house, usually
                         in the evening.

4  **Wean**              A young child.

5  **Footer, potter**   Fidget, rummage about.

6  **Cratur**            A creature. Used of a person, this could either be
                         a term of endearment or pity.

7  **Wan**               One.

8  **Bogie, bogey**      A low vehicle for moving material such as hay, coal, etc.

9  **Delph**             Delf china, glazed earthenware made at Delf (now Delft).

10 **Caldragh**          Graveyard for unbaptised children.

11 **Conacre**           Land let to a tenant for one season.

12 **Grape**             A four pronged fork.

13 **Haggard**           A stackyard (an area where hay is stored in stacks).

14 **Hut**               A stack of corn or hay, especially a small temporary stack.

15 **Wheen**             A few.

16 **Stirk**             A calf more than six and less than twelve months old.